MW01671977

UNIVERSITY ADMISSIONS MATH

SAT / ACT
Mathematics Primer

Second Edition

Jet Learning Laboratory

Jet Learning Laboratory JLL

Jet Learning Laboratory Inc. Publisher

Published by Jet Learning Laboratory, Inc.

ISBN-13: 978-0692265956

All inquiries should be addressed to:
Jet Learning Laboratory, Inc.
P.O. Box 52190
Houston, Texas 77052

PRINTED IN THE UNITED STATES OF AMERICA

To those champions that
study mathematics and science

CONTENTS

PREFACE

Universities and colleges must sort through thousands of applicant records from around the world that are representative of nearly as many unique high school teaching and grading standards. To help rapidly make sense of it all, colleges use standardized admissions testing. These tests, and additional tests, are also used to determine student placement and scholarship eligibility. The most popular standardized tests used for such purposes concerning college undergraduates are the SAT and ACT.

Math testing is often the most investigative testing at colleges, since student capabilities in mathematics largely predicts their initial success in first-year courses. To help maintain high retention rates in degree programs, students that are admitted to the college but that do not score above a certain threshold on mathematics admissions and supplemental placements tests are prohibited from officially enrolling in a major degree plan. Such students are required to take (i.e. pay for) mathematics courses at the college that do not count towards a degree. To continue at the college, and to be fully admitted into selective degree programs, students must pass such "developmental" courses covering lower level mathematics topics that the college ideally expected the in-coming students to have learned in high school. Large numbers of students may enter into developmental programs, spending money, including student loans, on college. However, student retention in such mathematics programs is generally low, resulting in a seeming epidemic of expensive discarded college dreams.

Mathematics admissions and placement testing also screen out some students that are the more gifted and talented in their high school class, graduating with high grades and honors. In such cases students may have experienced poor mathematics programs along their journey through elementary, middle, and high school. While innately gifted for mathematics, such students can have missed critical mathematics development phases, and as a result find it difficult to score in the high percentiles of the SAT or ACT regardless of how many practice tests that they take. In such cases, students miss-out on competitive scholarships and admission to their favorite University. Likewise, illnesses, family emergencies, natural disasters, and many other occurrences outside of a student's control can curtail certain mathematics skill development prior to entering college, limiting the student's mathematical maturity. However, specialized studying can help students close the knowledge and skills gap as evaluated by standardized admissions testing.

The mathematics lessons provided by this book guide you to a higher understanding and performance in the core mathematics that underlie all college admissions examinations concerning first-year undergraduate mathematics. While taking SAT and ACT practice tests can sometimes help improve a student's math score, such "practices" are test simulations and primarily contribute exposure to math problem styles, mostly benefitting students that have mastery over the core, and relatively static, underlying mathematics that constrain the tests. In other words, you have to have the ability to "ace" this book to have a shot at a high-percentile score on the SAT or ACT. So, start here, with *University Admissions Math*, and succeed while potentially saving yourself time and money.

The organization of the information guides you through math elements that are key to your understanding for both college and high school treatments of the essential algebra, geometry, and supporting mathematics topics underlying standardized mathematics admissions exams. As you understand such topics better, you will find that you can perform higher in complex problems and can learn new mathematics techniques with higher speed. That is where you want to be!

CHAPTER 1

How To Use This Book

This workbook is organized into four sections:

- A Brief SAT / ACT Math Diagnostic
- Let's Remember
- Guided Solutions By Objective
- Practice and Performance

A Brief SAT / ACT Math Diagnostic

The diagnostic is included to give you an opportunity to see how well you can perform on select SAT/ACT type problems. There are only 12 problems, so the diagnostic should take less that 10 minutes. However, you can allow up to 15 minutes. The answers to the diagnostic are provided at the end of the chapter. Your score is the percent out of 12 that you get correct. If you miss 2 or less, you score is greater than 80% and you are in pretty good shape.

Let's Remember

To use this workbook effectively, you should dive into the Let's Remember exercises. This section assumes that while you may not have a great understanding of how to do all of the problems correctly, you have significant successful experience working problems of these types. Primarily, you need to practice. If you feel that you understand certain problems well, still do them. All of them! Recognize that practicing something implies that you already have a good understanding. Practicing the math that you know is required to raise your proficiency. In other words, you practice to make math tests go "smoother" and "easier".

This section provides enough practice exercises to nominally demonstrate to yourself that you have the command of the required knowledge and skills. Here you can check your solution results with the answers provided at the end of the chapter for the odd numbered exercises. Where you are uncomfortable with problem, consult tutors, the internet, books, and any information source handy to help you improve your ability to perform the exercises.

Guided Solutions By Objective

This section provides exercises organized into 10 objectives. These problems are also generally "word problems". Such representations are the problem types generally reported as the biggest challenge for students during exams. The underlying mathematics is key, and hints are provided to jog your intuition and memory. Utilize the hints to help you learn the key thought patterns for resolving each particular problem.

Detailed solutions for each problem are provided at the end of each objective section. Repeat the problems that you solved incorrectly using the detailed solutions. Even if you copy the solution step-by-step, the practice of actually performing the problem with your own hands and mind provides you with critical proficiency training. Also, if you simply guessed the correct answer for a problem, repeat the problem using the detailed solution.

Also, in the margin provided, include you own notes along way as you progress through the lessons.

Practice and Performance

Two exams are provided. The first exam should be taken without regard to a time limit. The answers are provided following the exam. You should score yourself two points for every correct answer. A score of 80 or better is a good score. Regardless of your score, you should go back through the material and examine how to correctly perform the problems that you missed or skipped. Concentrate not only on the answer, but seek to understand the correct procedure. Review related exercises from the Guided Solutions By Objective chapter, as well as other sources.

The second exam should be taken with a time limit of 70 minutes (1 hour and 10 minutes). In this case score yourself using the answer key given, assigning two points for each correct answer. A score of 80 or better is a good score. Also, review all questions where your response is incorrect.

After completing this workbook, store it for a couple of weeks, then pull it out again and review the all of work that you have done – from the beginning. You will find that it is easy to follow what you have done and such reviewing exercise will cause you to gain a deeper connection to the mathematics.

Feels Good! – Now, You Want More

Congratulations on your progress! Check your bookstores for more great JLL products. Also, when you have questions about JLL products or desire more insight and information on mathematics and science learning, interact with us online (e.g. www.facebook.com/jetlearninglaboratory, www.twitter,com/NewsJLL, www.jetlearninglaboratory.com) and via email (hiJLL@jetlearninglaboratory.com).

CHAPTER 2

A Brief SAT / ACT Math Diagnostic

The following 12 problems comprise a brief diagnostic to help you calibrate your current readiness for the SAT and ACT. The questions are typical of both examinations, where the level of difficulty present is representative of about midway through an SAT Math section or the later half of the ACT Math examination.

You should do the problems in any order that you like, taking no more that 15 minutes. You should do the problems in one sitting and not utilize any references, assistance from tutors, or other help. You may use a calculator.

After You Complete The Diagnostic

With the diagnostic exam completed, compare your answer selections to the answers provide at the end of this Chapter and calculate a percentage score = number correct / 12 * 100.

If you score 80% or better, then you may have a good mathematics background for the SAT or ACT. You can complete the 2 exams at the end of this book for more practice, and then pick up a reference of practice SAT or ACT problems for more exposure to different problem styles.

If you score less that 80% you should review the problems to see if having the answer jogs your memory of how to reduce the problems to the correct answers. The detailed explanations for the correct results are not provided, to keep you from fooling yourself into thinking that you understand the underlying methodology simply because you can read the solution. If the problem solution paths do not come to you during a brief review of the correct answers, then there are significant mathematics gaps. Such gaps are not efficiently closed by attempting lots of SAT or ACT practice examinations, since you may be stumped too often and, for a substantial number of the problems, simply skip or blindly guess. Start this book at Chapter 3 and complete all the lessons to increase you capabilities.

The Diagnostic

1) $\frac{\frac{mx}{yz}}{\frac{yx}{mz}} =$

A. $\frac{x^2}{z^2}$ B. m^2z^2 C. $\frac{m^2}{y^2}$ D. 1 E. $\frac{1}{m^2z^2}$

2) Kim's chain of healthy cupcake shops sold 2,105,000 cupcakes in 2012. If her stores sold only 1,914,250 cupcakes in 2013, by what percent did the number of cupcakes sold decrease?

A. 96%
B. 6.4%
C. 1%
D. 31%
E. 5%

3) Four liters of a candy mixture is made up of 7 parts melted fudge and 3 parts liquid caramel. If a new candy is to be manufactured that requires the mixture to be adjusted to 40% caramel, how many liters of caramel must be added to the original mixture?

A. $2\frac{1}{2}$ liters
B. 4 liters
C. $1\frac{1}{4}$ liters
D. $1\frac{2}{3}$ liters
E. $\frac{1}{2}$ liters

4) The average of 6, 2, n, and n is 14. The average of 10, 3, m, and n is 24. m = ?

A. 3
B. 10
C. 14
D. 8
E. 11

5) Consider the set S: {6, -4, 0, 14, 4, x} where is a real number. For which of the following values of x is the median of the set S equal to 5?

A. 5
B. 7
C. 2
D. -1
E. 4

6) $\frac{1}{4}$ is what percent of $(\sqrt{5})^3$?

A. 5
B. 50
C. .25
D. 25
E. $\sqrt{5}$

7) If $\frac{x-1}{y-1} = \frac{y}{x}$ then x+y =

A. 1
B. 2
C. 0.5
D. 0
E. Cannot be determined from the given information

8) If 6m – 2n = 4 and m + 3n = 24, then 5(m - n) =

A. 14
B. 0
C. 2
D. -15
E. -20

9) If $4x - 14 < 2y + 6$ and $3x + 4 > y$, and x is greater than 2 and less than 3, then y could be

A. 8
B. 9
C. 10
D. 13
E. 14

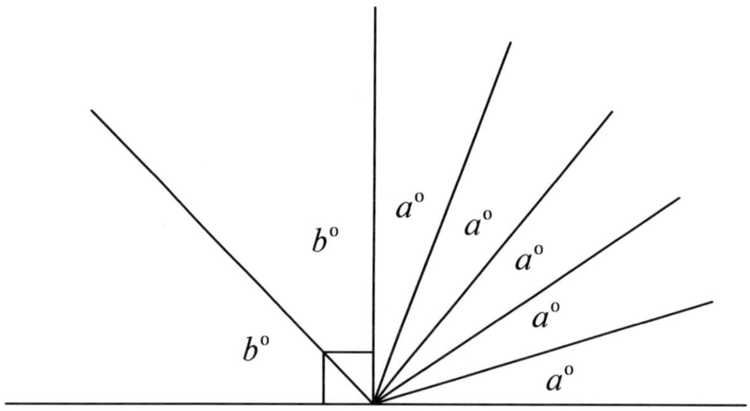

10. In the figure above, what is the value of $11a - 3b$?

A. 63º
B. 45º
C. 98º
D. 129º
E. 112º

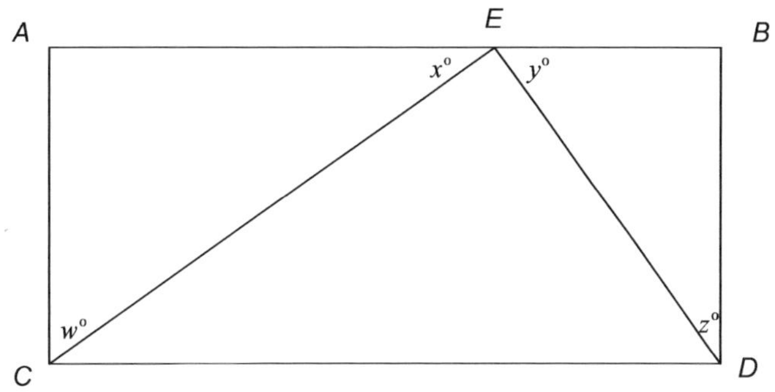

11. If ABCD is a rectangle, what is the value of $w+x+y+z$?

A. 180
B. 200
C. 240
D. 270
E. 135

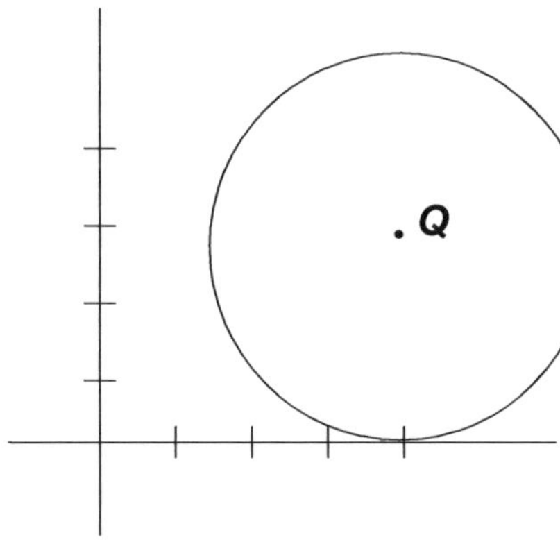

12. Center Q of the circle above has coordinates of $(4,\ 3)$. What is the area of the circle?

A. 4π
B. 36π
C. 9π
D. 7π
E. 49π

Answers To The Diagnostic

1) C; 2) E; 3) D; 4) D; 5) B; 6) E; 7) A; 8) E; 9) B; 10) A; 11) A; 12) C

CHAPTER 3

LET'S REMEMBER

Practice Fraction Operations

1. $\frac{6}{7}+\frac{1}{7}=$ $\frac{7}{7}=1$
2. $\frac{5}{6}+\frac{1}{6}=$ $\frac{6}{6}=1$
3. $\frac{7}{8}+\frac{3}{4}=$
4. $\frac{1}{2}+\frac{4}{8}=$
5. $\frac{1}{5}+\frac{1}{10}=$
6. $\frac{4}{9}+\frac{2}{2}=$
7. $\frac{1}{3}+\frac{2}{5}=$
8. $\frac{2}{3}+\frac{1}{4}=$
9. $\frac{4}{8}-\frac{3}{4}=$
10. $\frac{1}{6}-\frac{1}{5}=$
11. $\frac{2}{5}-\frac{1}{4}=$
12. $\frac{1}{20}-\frac{1}{10}=$
13. $\frac{7}{8}-\frac{5}{6}=$
14. $\frac{4}{5}-\frac{1}{3}=$
15. $\frac{8}{9}-\frac{3}{7}=$
16. $\frac{7}{10}-\frac{1}{8}=$
17. $\frac{1}{4}\times\frac{5}{12}=$
18. $\frac{4}{3}\times\frac{12}{9}=$
19. $\frac{2}{4}\times\frac{2}{10}=$
20. $\frac{3}{5}\times\frac{4}{5}=$
21. $\frac{3}{4}\times\frac{1}{3}=$
22. $\frac{6}{10}\times\frac{3}{5}=$
23. $\frac{3}{4}\times\frac{8}{9}=$
24. $\frac{4}{5}\times\frac{3}{4}=$
25. $\frac{2}{6}\div\frac{5}{12}=$
26. $\frac{5}{8}\div\frac{2}{4}=$
27. $\frac{8}{9}\div\frac{3}{4}=$

Express the following as fractions

1. 0.1
2. 0.4
3. 0.11
4. 0.01
5. 0.45
6. 0.80
7. 0.88
8. 0.30
9. 0.35
10. 0.75
11. 0.25
12. 0.025
13. 0.0025
14. 0.002
15. 0.006
16. 0.018
17. 0.12
18. 0.9
19. 0.95
20. 3.15
21. 2.25
22. 4.60

SOLVE FOR X

1. $5x = 15$
2. $10x = 50$
3. $7x = 63$
4. $2x = 200$
5. $12x = 60$
6. $7x = 49$
7. $6x = 30$
8. $8x = 72$
9. $4x = 32$
10. $3x = 54$
11. $\frac{3}{2}x = \frac{1}{3}$
12. $\frac{1}{4}x = \frac{1}{3}$
13. $\frac{2}{7}x = \frac{1}{2}$
14. $\frac{3}{4}x = \frac{1}{2}$
15. $\frac{4}{2}x = \frac{1}{4}$
16. $\frac{4}{5}x = \frac{3}{1}$
17. $\frac{1}{3}x = 3$
18. $\frac{1}{5}x = 5$
19. $\frac{2}{3}x = 7$
20. $\frac{3}{6}x = 6$
21. $6x = 84$

MORE: SOLVE FOR X

1. $4x - 11 = 17$

2. $\frac{1}{2}x - 14 = {}^{-}1$

3. $4x + 2 = 14$

4. $3x + 6 = 12$

5. $4x + 4 = {}^{-}2x - 8$

6. $2x + 4 = {}^{-}6$

7. ${}^{-}2x + 7 = 7$

8. $2x + 8 = 40$

9. $3(x - 4) = 2x + 6$

10. $3x - 15 = 33$

11. $6x + 3 = 4x + 9$

12. $40x - 3 = 2$

13. $6x + \frac{1}{3} = \frac{1}{3}$

14. $\frac{-1}{7}x + 3 = {}^{-}2$

15. $4x + 3 = {}^{-}5$

16. $10 - 8x = 2(5 - 4x)$

17. $\frac{1}{3}x - 18 = 7$

18. $\frac{-1}{8}x + 4 = 13$

19. $\frac{-1}{8}x - 4 = 3$

20. $4x - 15 = 9$

21. $^{-}5x + 7 = 62$

22. $20x + 5 = 105$

23. $\frac{1}{10}x - 5 = 9$

24. $7x - 6 = ^{-}104$

25. $^{-}6x + 2 = ^{-}4$

26. $\frac{1}{2}x + 5 = ^{-}12$

27. $\frac{1}{2}x + 4 = 20$

28. $\frac{1}{3}x + 2 = 6$

29. $56x + 12 = 112$

30. $5x - 9 = 2$

Percent

1. Find 50% of 88.

2. What number is 15% of 40?

3. Find 5% of 160.

4. What number is 80% of 20?

5. Find 6% of 90.

6. What number is 18% of 90?

7. Find 3% of 12.

8. What number is 60% of 120?

9. Find 11% of 121.

10. What number is 27% of 120%?

11. Find 98% of 65.

12. What number is 20% of 80?

13. Find 15% of 45.

14. What is 8% of 25?

15. Find 30% of 40.

16. What number is 25% of 95?

17. Find 20% of 20.

18. What number is 30% of 120?

19. Find 12% of 33.

20. What number is 120% of 34?

Finding the Slope and Y-intercept Of a Line

Find the slope of the following lines.

1. $(-5,6)\,(3,2)$

2. $(-1,-2)\,(0,-5)$

3. $(-5,-2)\,(-3,5)$

4. $(-6,7)\,(-5,0)$

5. $(5,3)\,(-2,1)$

6. $(-5,7)\,(-3,1)$

7. $(1,2,)\,(3,4)$

8. $(-1,-1)\,(-5,5)$

9. $(-5,8)\,(2,0)$

10. $(4,5)\,(-3,7)$

Write the equation of the line with the given slope and point

11. $m = -2\ (-5, 6)$

12. $m = 3\ (-2, 0)$

13. $m = \frac{1}{2}\ (0, -5)$

14. $m = \frac{2}{3}\ (-3, 8)$

15. $m = -5\ (2, 1)$

Write the equation of the line that passes through the given points

16. $(3, 8)(4, 3)$

17. $(3, 10)(-1, 0)$

18. $(-3, -1)(-1, 0)$

19. $(1, 5)(07)$

20. $(-8, 4)(2, 7)$

21. $(6, -1)(-2, 1)$

Linear Inequalities

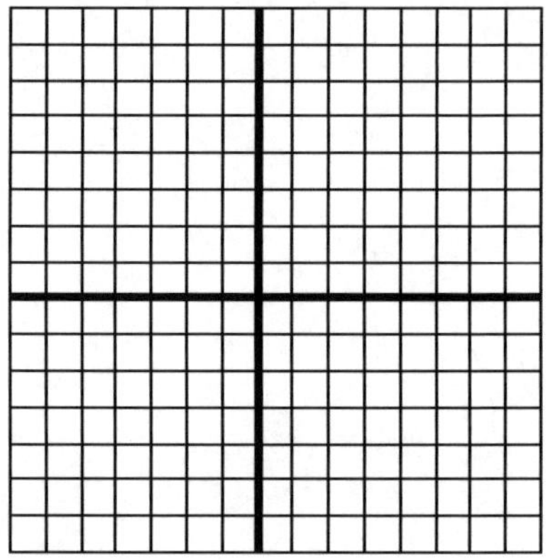

1. Graph the inequality $3x - 2y < 12$ for y.

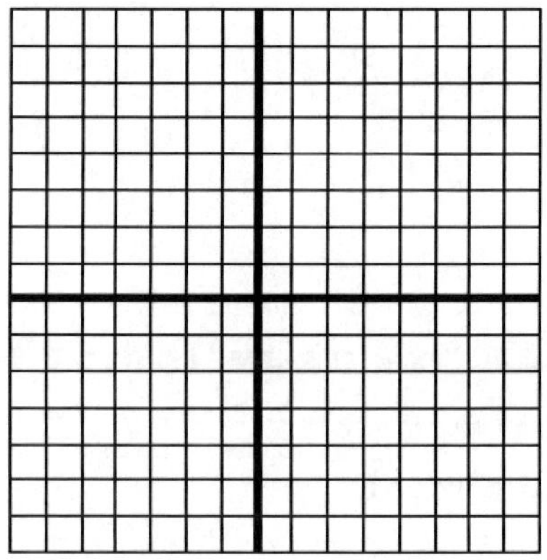

Graph each inequality.

2. $y \geq x + 1$

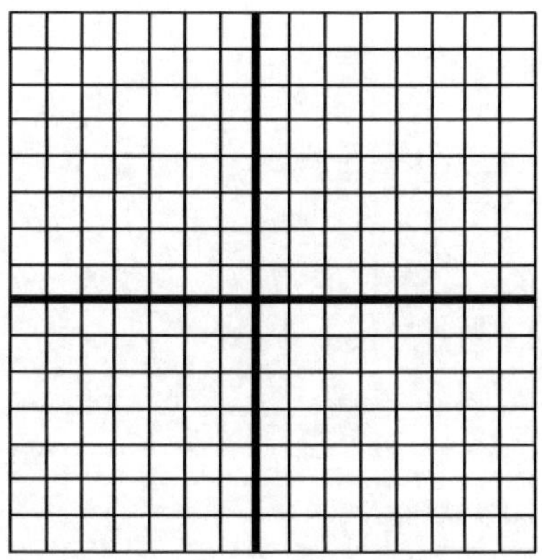

3. $x + y \leq 3$

4. $2x - 5y < 20$

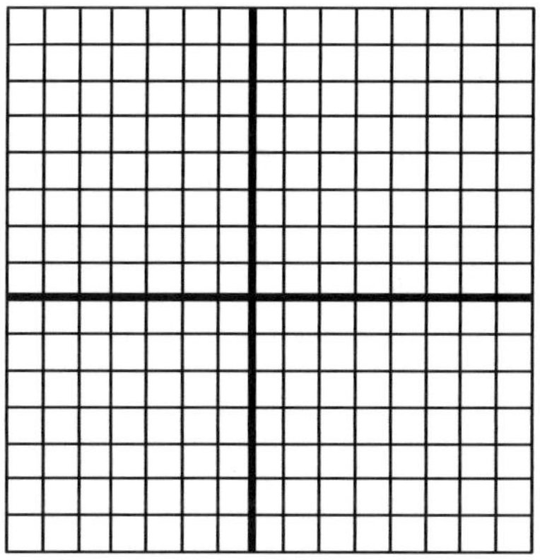

5. $y > 2$

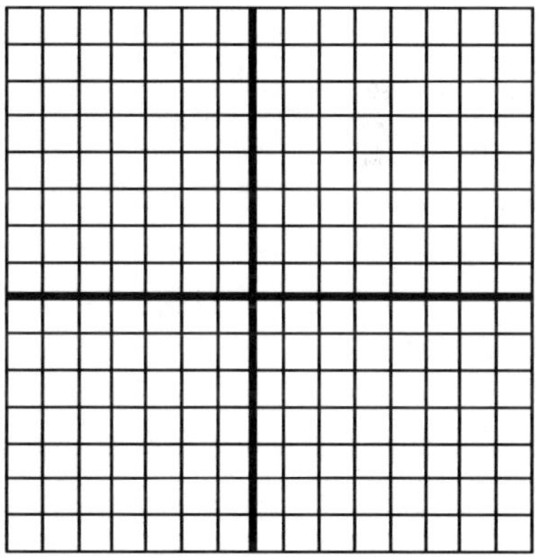

6. $x \geq -1$

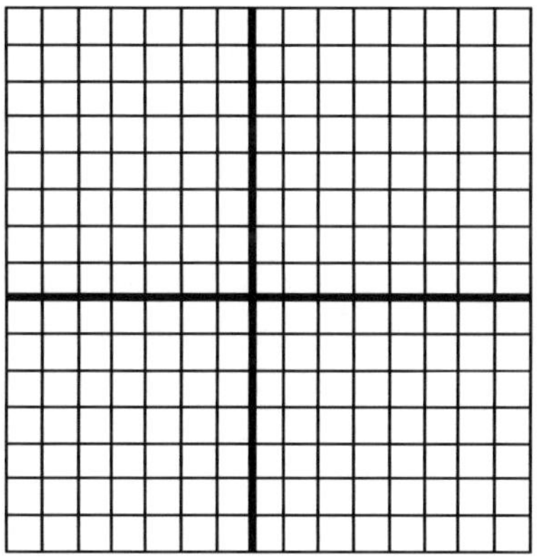

7. $y \geq 2x$

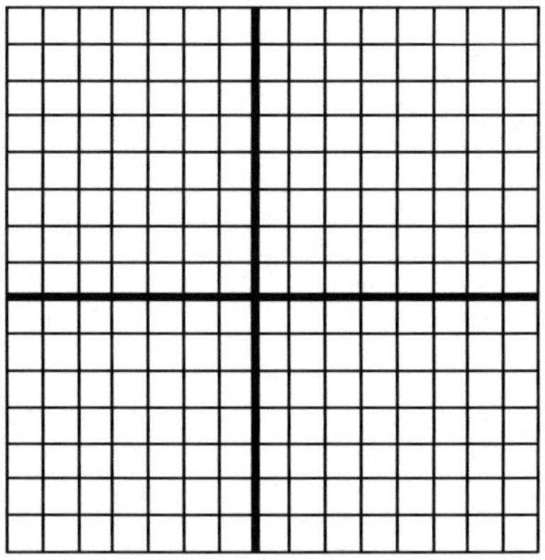

8. $y < 3x$

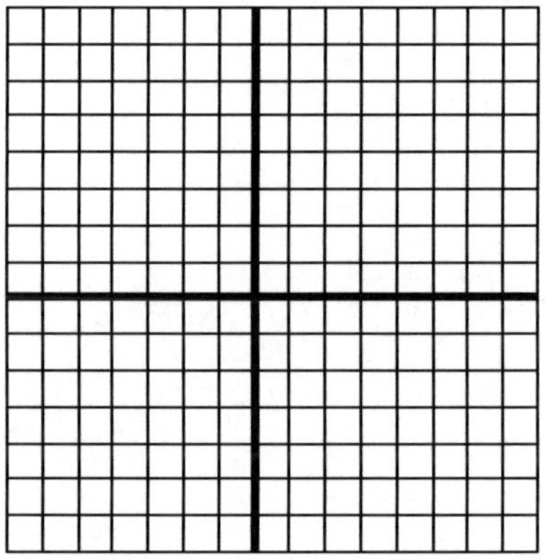

9. $y \leq 2x - 1$

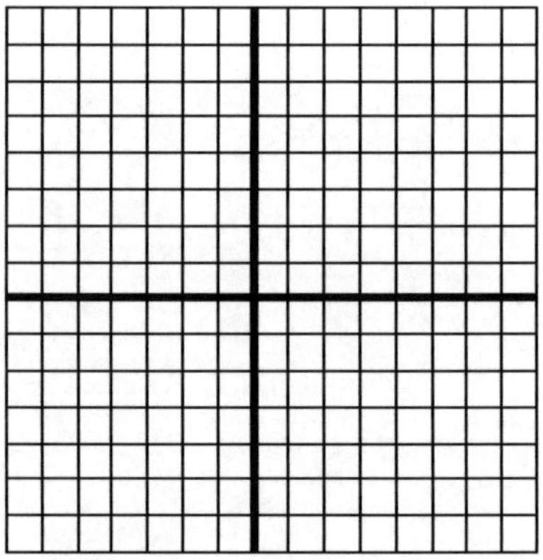

Systems of Inequalities

Graph each system of inequalities.

1. $x \geq 3$
   $y \leq 5$

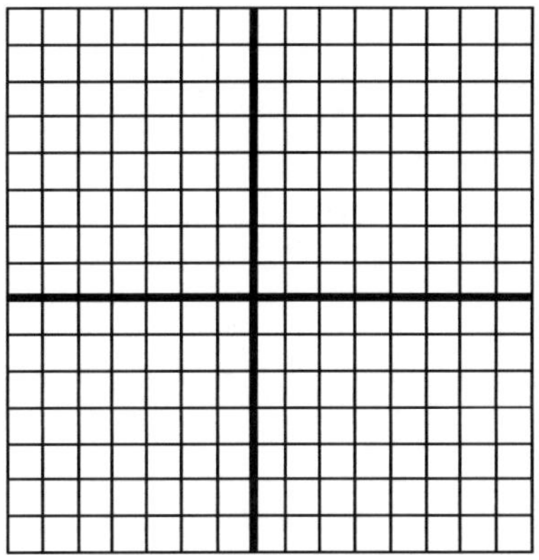

2. $y > x$
   $y > 0$

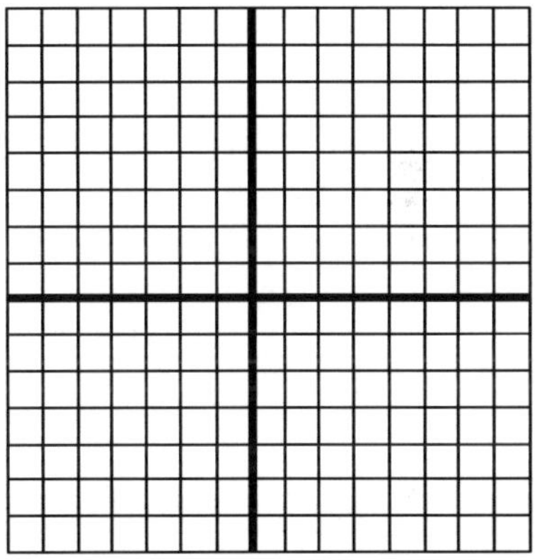

3. $y < x + 4$
   $y \geq -2x + 2$

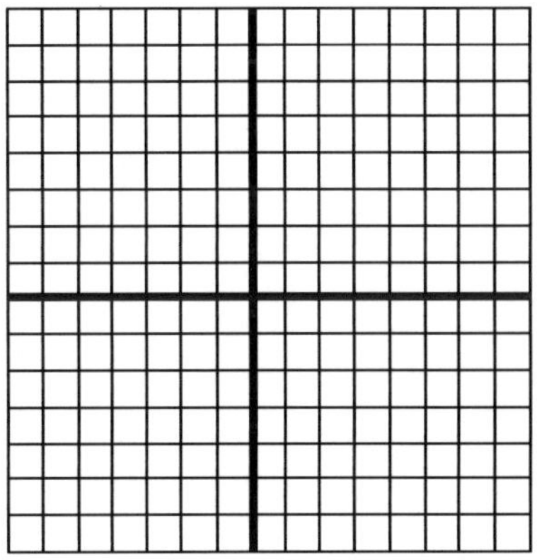

4. $\begin{aligned} 2x - y &\geq 4 \\ x + y &\leq 3 \end{aligned}$

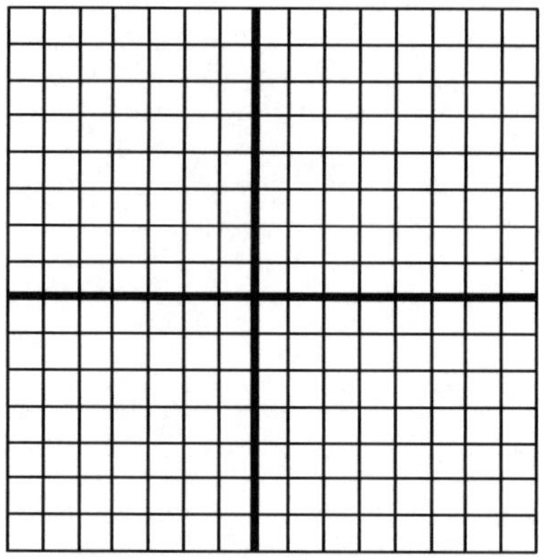

5. $\begin{aligned} y &\geq 0 \\ x &\geq -2 \end{aligned}$

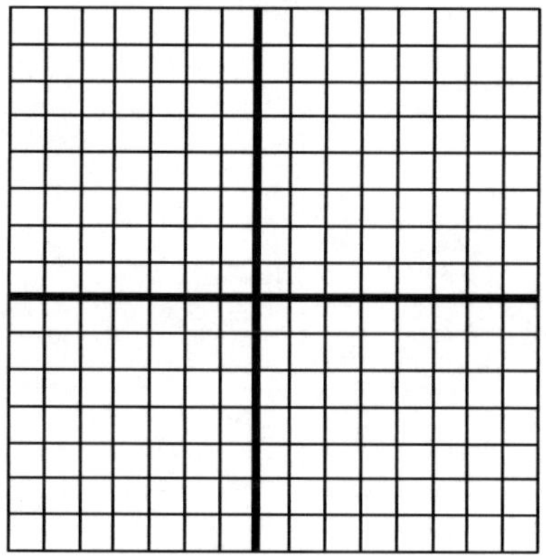

6. $\begin{aligned} x &< 0 \\ y &> \frac{1}{2}x \end{aligned}$

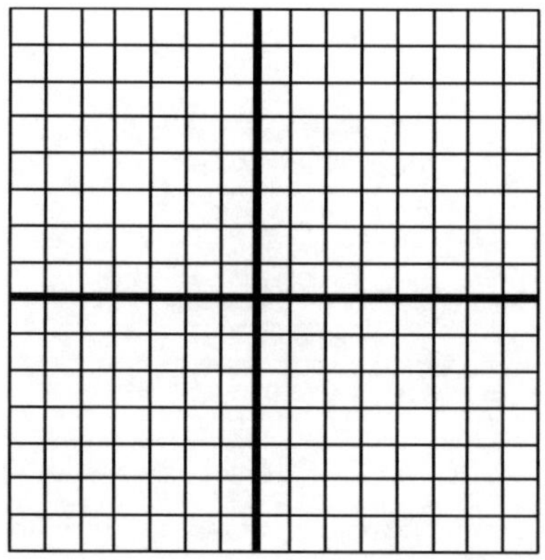

Try These

1. $\frac{5}{7}+\frac{3}{7}=$

2. $\frac{3}{5}+\frac{1}{2}=$

3. $\frac{2}{6}\times\frac{3}{9}=$

4. $\frac{5}{12}\times\frac{4}{7}=$

5. $\frac{1}{5}\div\frac{3}{6}=$

6. $\frac{12}{13}\div\frac{4}{8}=$

Solve for *x* in the following.

7. $5x-13=-2$

8. $40x-2=3$

9. Define the slope of a line? How many points (coordinates) do you need to calculate the slope of a straight line?

10. How many points are required to define a straight line?

11. If the slope of a straight line is known, how many points are required to specify the equation of the line?

12. $2x-3x(2x-y)=$

13. $2x+5x+6y-y+2xy=$

Graph the line that contains the point and has the given slope.

14. point: $(-1, 3)$; slope: 3

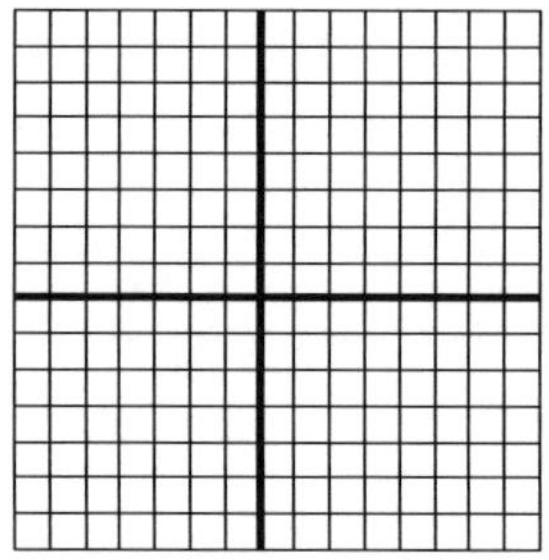

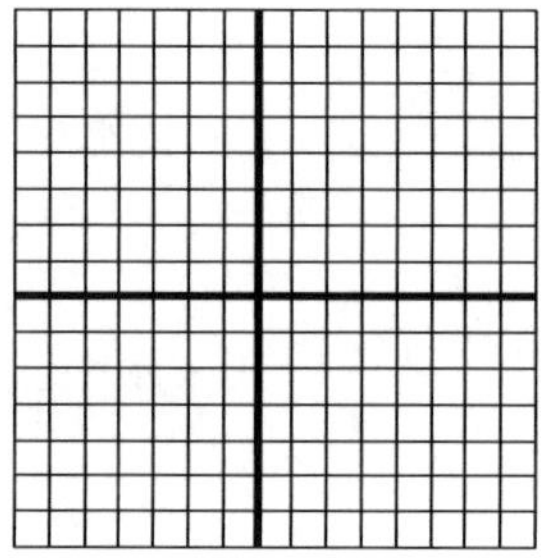

15. point: $(0, 3)$; slope: -5

Write an equation of a line through the given points.

16. $(3,-3)$, $(-3, 1)$

17. $(7, 3)$, $(2, 2)$

18. You have 35 questions correct in a high school math exit test of 50 questions. What percent of the questions were correct?

19. The price of a gallon of gasoline was \$1.55 last year. It increased to \$2.95 this month. Find the percent of increase.

20. The annual budget for medical research at a local hospital was \$1,500,000 last year. The budget is \$900,000 this year. What is the percent of decrease?

21. What number is 15% of 45?

Try Again

Graph the line that contains the point and has the given slope.

1. point: (4, 3); slope: $-\frac{2}{3}$

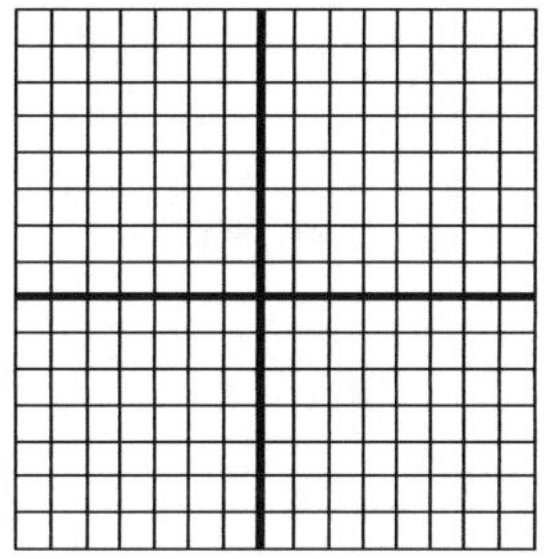

2. point: (1, 0); slope: 2

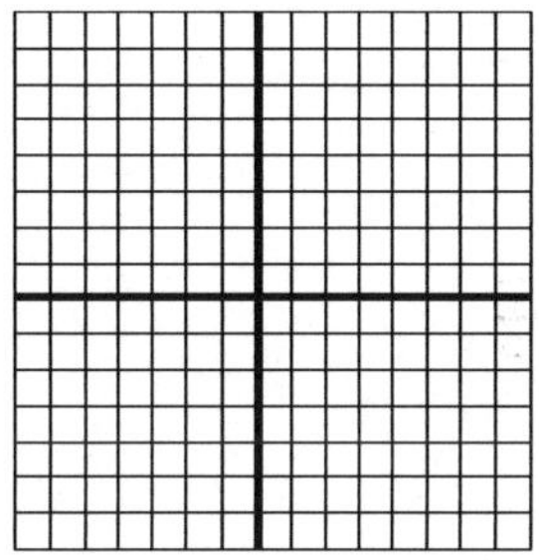

Write an equation of a line through the given points.

3. (2,2), (– 12, 14)

4. (7, 21), (7, -7)

5.

a. $\frac{7}{8} - \frac{5}{6} =$

b. $\frac{4}{5} - \frac{1}{3} =$

c. $\frac{8}{9} - \frac{3}{7} =$

d. $\frac{7}{10} - \frac{1}{8} =$

e. $\frac{1}{4} \times \frac{5}{12} =$

f. $\frac{4}{3} \times \frac{12}{9} =$

6. Jason paid a down payment of $24 for a jacket. The down payment is 10% of the price. What is the price of the jacket?

7. Which of the following equations has a graph that is a parabola?

A. $y = 3x$ B. $y = 3x^2$ C. $y = 2x^3$

Express each product.

8. $(y+3)^2$

9. $(r-4)^2$

10. $(2p+1)^2$

11. $(3+\sqrt{5})^2$

12. $(x+6)(x-6)$

13. $(3n-2)(3n+2)$

The Quadratic Formula

Quadratic Formula: $x = \dfrac{-b \pm \sqrt{b^2 - 4ac}}{2a}$

Based on the standard form $ax^2 + bx + c = 0$, identify the values of a, b, and c.

1. $x^2 + 16x + 64 = 0$

2. $x^2 - 3x - 10 = 0$

3. $5x^2 - x + 1 = 0$

4. $x^2 + 2x = 35$

Rewrite each equation in the form $ax^2 + bx + c = 0$. Then solve.

5. $x^2 + 3x - 6 = 3$

6. $4x^2 - 2x = 1$

7. $x^2 + 6 = 8x$

8. $25x^2 = 6x$

Solve each equation using the quadratic formula.

9. $x^2 - 3x - 8 = 0$

10. $x^2 - 6x + 5 = 0$

11. $x^2 - 10x + 1 = 0$

12. $x^2 + 4x + 3 = 0$

13. $x^2 + 11x - 3 = 0$

14. $x^2 - 12x = 0$

Using the Discriminant

The expression $b^2 - 4ac$ in the quadratic formula is called the **discriminant.** The discriminant gives you information about the number of possible solutions when you solve a quadratic equation.

Example	Value of $b^2 - 4ac$	Discriminant a Perfect Square?	Nature of Root (s)
1	$b^2 - 4ac > 0$	Yes	2 real, rational
2	$b^2 - 4ac > 0$	No	2 real, irrational
3	$b^2 - 4ac < 0$	-	2 imaginary
4	$b^2 - 4ac = 0$	-	1 real

For each equation, find the number of solutions.

1. $x^2 - 8x + 12 = 0$

2. $3x^2 - x + 3 = 0$

3. $x^2 + 6x + 9 = 0$

4. $3x^2 - x + 15 = 0$

5. $-2x^2 - 5x + 4 = 0$

6. $15x^2 - 10x = 0$

7. $5x^2 - 18 = -30$

8. $x^2 - 49 = 0$

Try Exponents

Rewrite each product using exponents.

1. $-(9\cdot 9\cdot 9\cdot 9\cdot 9\cdot 9\cdot 9\cdot 9\cdot 9\cdot 9)$

2. $xy\cdot xy\cdot xy\cdot xy\cdot xy$

3. $3(\frac{1}{4}\cdot\frac{1}{4}\cdot\frac{1}{4}\cdot\frac{1}{4}\cdot\frac{1}{4}\cdot\frac{1}{4}\cdot\frac{1}{4}\cdot\frac{1}{4})$

Evaluate each power.

1. 2^5

2. $(\frac{1}{2})^3$

3. $(-3)^4$

Evaluate each expression when x=2 and y=5.

1. $3x^5+10$
2. $6y^2-x^4$
3. $4(2-y)^3$
4. x^4y
5. xy^3
6. $(xy)^3$
7. x^4+y^4
8. $(x+y)^4$
9. y^x
10. x^y
11. $10(x-y)^3$
12. $(x-y)^2y^3$

Simplify each expression.

13. 11^{-2}

14. 0.747966^{0}

15. $(9^{0})(7^{-2})$

16. $(\frac{1}{5})^{-2}$

17. 13^{0}

18. 5^{-6}

19. $(\frac{1}{5})^{0}$

20. $(\frac{3}{5})^{-3}$

21. $(\frac{2}{3})^{-4}$

22. $\frac{1}{4^{0}}$

ANSWERS TO ODD NUMBERED QUESTIONS

(YOUR NOTES)

ANSWERS TO ODD NUMBERED QUESTIONS

Practice Fraction Problems

prob	ans	prob	ans
1	1	15	$29/63$
3	$13/8$	17	$5/48$
5	$3/10$	19	$1/10$
7	$11/15$	21	14
9	$-1/3$	23	$2/3$
11	$3/20$	25	$4/5$
13	$1/24$	27	$32/27$

Express The Following As Fractions

prob	ans	prob	ans
1	$1/10$	13	$1/400$
3	$11/100$	15	$3/500$
5	$9/20$	17	$3/25$
7	$22/25$	19	$19/20$
9	$7/20$	21	$9/4$
11	$1/4$		

ANSWERS TO ODD NUMBERED QUESTIONS (continued)

Solve For X

prob	ans	prob	ans
1	3	**13**	$7/4$
3	9	**15**	$1/8$
5	5	**17**	9
7	5	**19**	$21/2$
9	8	**21**	14
11	$2/9$		

More Solve For X

1	7	**9**	18
3	3	**11**	3
5	-2	**13**	0
7	0	**15**	-2
17	75	**25**	1
19	-56	**27**	32
21	-11	**29**	$25/14$
23	140		

Percents

prob	ans	prob	ans
1	44	**11**	63.7
3	8	**13**	6.75
5	5.4	**15**	12
7	0.36	**17**	4
9	13.31	**19**	3.96

ANSWERS TO ODD NUMBERED QUESTIONS (continued)

Finding The Slope And Y-Intercept Of Line

prob	ans
1	$-1/2$
3	$7/2$
5	$2/7$
7	1
9	$-8/7$
11	$y = -2x - 4$
13	$y = -\frac{1}{2}x - 5$
15	$y = -5x + 11$
17	$y = -5x + 23$
19	$y = -2x + 7$
21	$y = -\frac{1}{4}x + \frac{1}{2}$

ANSWERS TO ODD NUMBERED QUESTIONS (continued)

Linear Inequalities

2. $3x - 2y < 12$ for y.

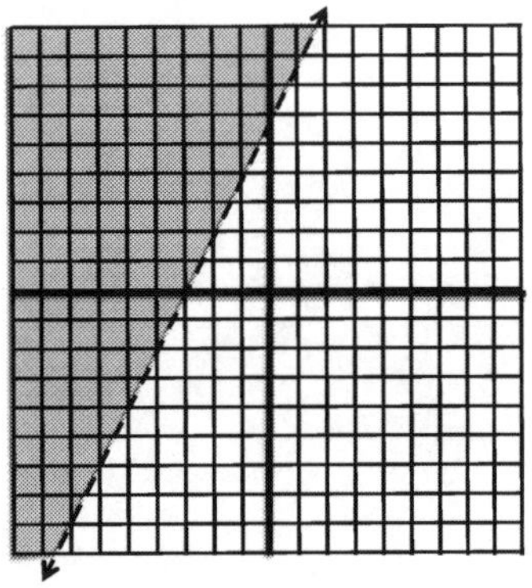

3. $x + y \leq 3$

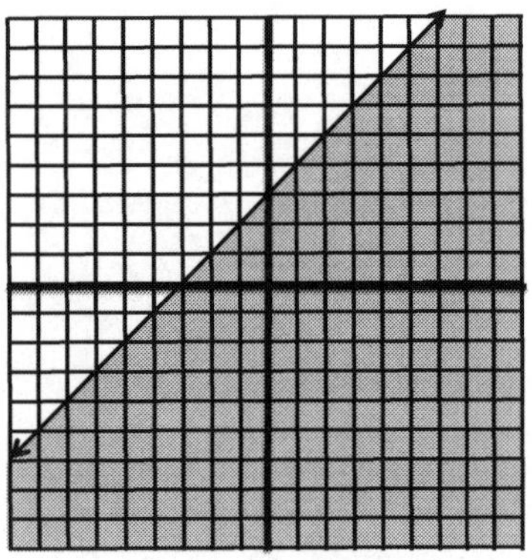

5. $y > 2$

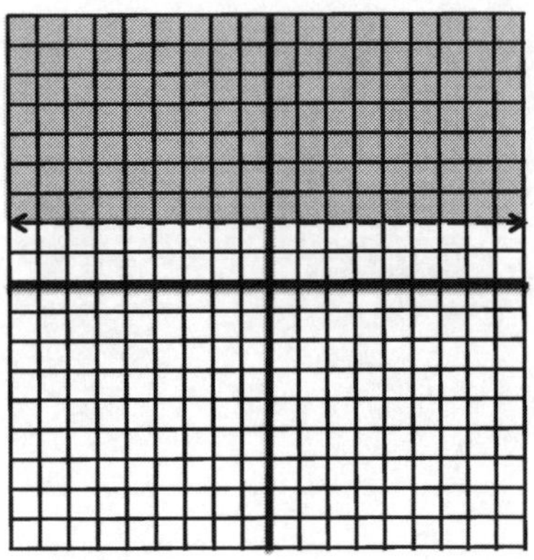

ANSWERS TO ODD NUMBERED QUESTIONS (continued)

7. $y \geq 2x$

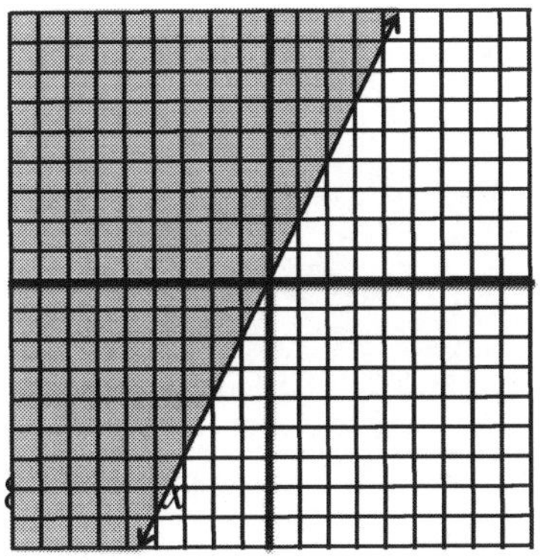

9. $y \leq 2x - 1$

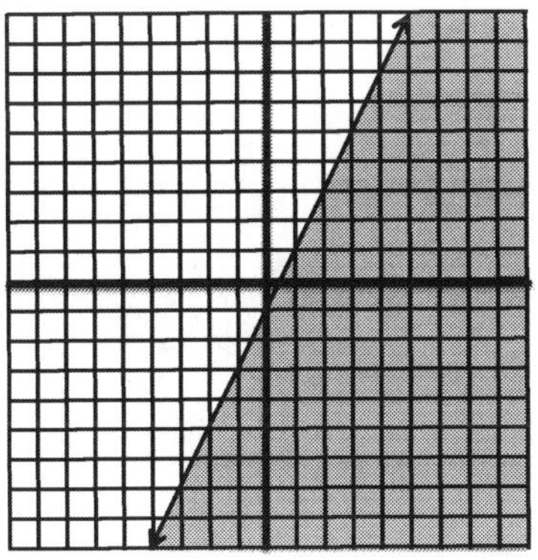

ANSWERS TO ODD NUMBERED QUESTIONS (continued)

Systems Of Inequalities

1. $x \geq 3, \ y \leq 5$

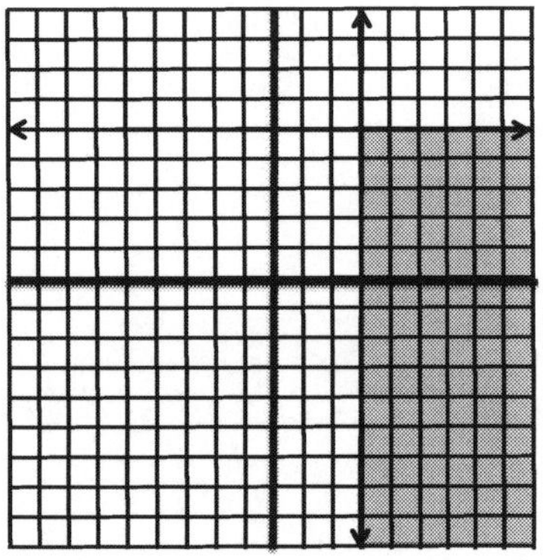

3. $y < x + 4, \quad y \geq -2x + 2$

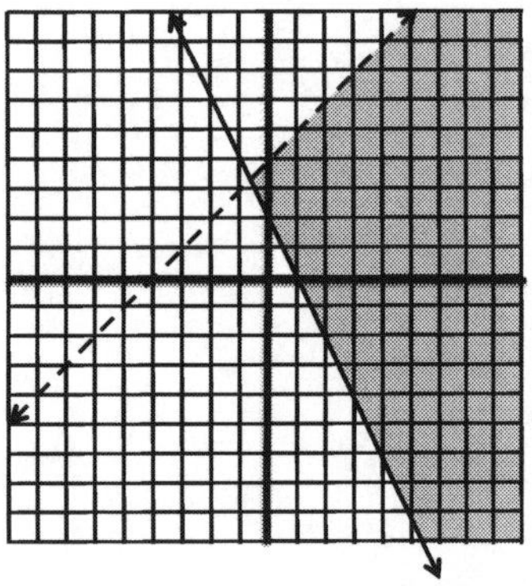

5. $y \geq 0, \quad x \geq -2$

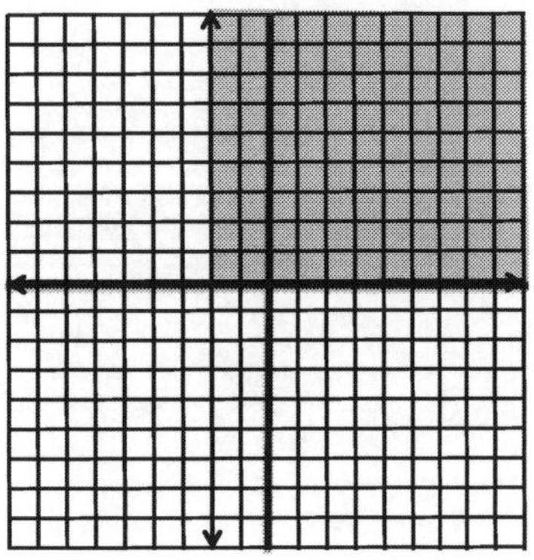

ANSWERS TO ODD NUMBERED QUESTIONS (continued)

TRY THESE

1 $\frac{8}{7}$

3 $\frac{1}{9}$

5 $\frac{2}{5}$

7 $\frac{5}{11}$

9 The inclination of the line (rise over run).

11 1 point

13 7x-5y+2xy

15. point: (0, 3); slope: -5

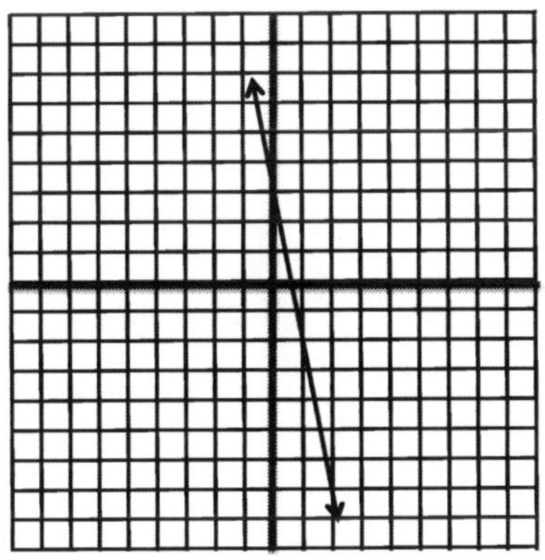

17. $y = \frac{1}{5}x + \frac{8}{5}$

19. 90.3%

21. 6.74

ANSWERS TO ODD NUMBERED QUESTIONS (continued)

Try Again

1. point: (4, 3); slope: $-\frac{2}{3}$

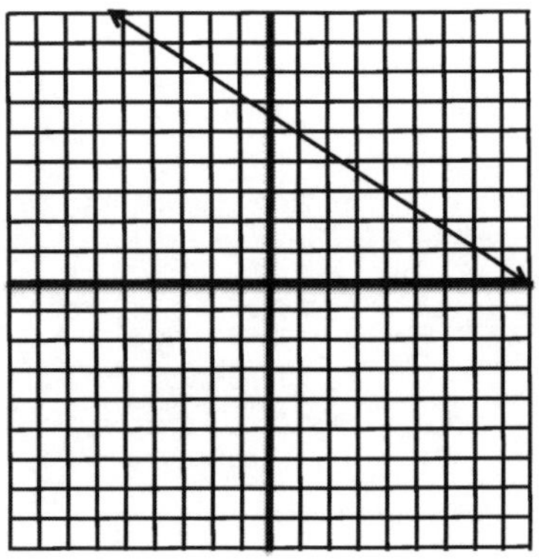

3. $y = \frac{-6}{7}x + \frac{26}{7}$

5.

$a.\ ^{1}/_{24},\ b.\ ^{7}/_{17},\ c.\ ^{29}/_{63}$

$d.\ ^{23}/_{40},\ e.\ ^{5}/_{48},\ f.\ ^{16}/_{9}$

7. B.
9. $r^2 - 8r + 16$
11. $14 + 6\sqrt{5}$
13. $9n^2 - 4$

ANSWERS TO ODD NUMBERED QUESTIONS (continued)

The Quadratic Formula

1 a=1, b =16, c=64

3 a=5, b=-1, c=1

5

$$x^2 + 3x - 9 = 0,$$
$$x = \frac{-3}{2} \pm \frac{9\sqrt{5}}{2}$$

7

$$x^2 - 8x + 6 = 0,$$
$$x = 4 \pm \sqrt{10}$$

9

$$x = \frac{3}{2} \pm \frac{\sqrt{41}}{2}$$

11

$$x = 5 \pm 2\sqrt{6}$$

13

$$x = \frac{-11}{2} \pm \frac{\sqrt{33}}{2}$$

Using The Discriminant

1. 2 real solutions
3. 1 real solution
5. 2 real solutions
7. no real solutions

ANSWERS TO ODD NUMBERED QUESTIONS (continued)

Try Exponents

1. -9^{10}

3. $3\left(\frac{1}{4}\right)^8$

Evaluate each power.

1. 32, 3. 81

Evaluate each expression when x=2 and y=5.

1. 106
3. -108
5. 250
7. 641
9. 25
11. -270
13. $\frac{1}{121}$
15. $\frac{1}{49}$
17. 1
19. 1
21. $\frac{81}{16}$

CHAPTER 4

GUIDED SOLUTIONS BY OBJECTIVE

Objective 1: Functional Relationships

Question 1

Which of the following does not represent a function?

A. $\{(-2,3)(2,3)(3,-2)(0,0)\}$

B. $\{(0,-1)(2,3)(-2,-3)(1,5)\}$

C.

x	y
0	2
-1	3
-2	3
0	5
1	6
2	4
3	6

D.

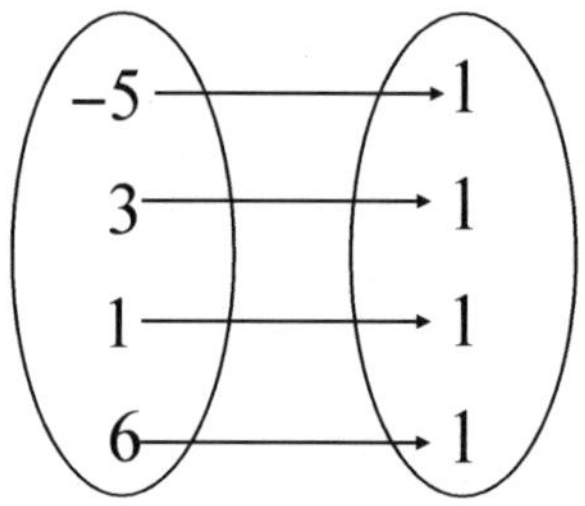

Your Notes

Hint: Remember that a function does not have repeating x values that correspond to different y values.

Question 2

Which equation does not represent a functional relationship?

A. $-y = -x$

B. $x = -2$

C. $y = 3$

D. $y = x^2 - x$

Hint: Refer to the hint from question number one.

Question 3

Bambi Movies rents movies for a fee of \$2.25 per day. Name the independent variable in this situation.

A. The number of days the movie is rented

B. The total charge once the movie is returned

C. Name of the movie

D. The cost per day to rent a movie

Your Notes

Hint: The independent variable is the variable that is arbitrarily specified in a functional relationship.

Question 4

Which of the following equations best represents the graph shown below?

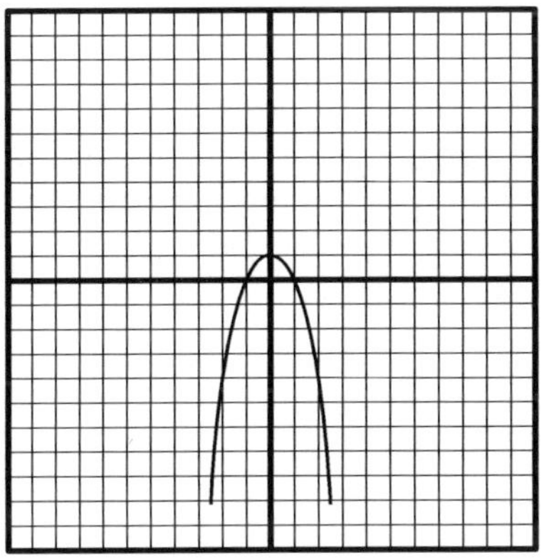

A. A linear function with the equation $y = -x + 1$

B. A quadratic function with the equation $y = x^2 + 1$

C. An absolute value function with the equation $y = -|x - 1|$

D. A quadratic function with the equation $y = -x^2 + 1$

Hint: The graph shown is a parabola. Determine whether the parabola shown above opens in the negative or positive direction.

Question 5

Which of the following inequalities best describes the graph shown below?

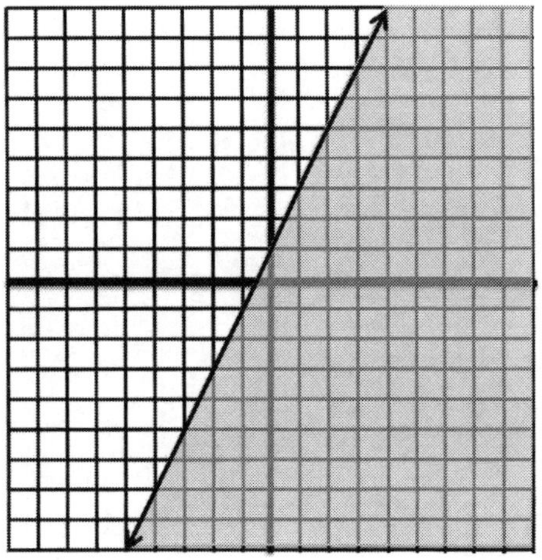

A. $y < -2x + 1$

B. $y < 2x + 1$

C. $y \geq 2x + 1$

D. $y \leq 2x + 1$

Your Notes

Hint: The graph has a solid line to include the equality, i.e. "less than or equal to" or "greater than or equal to".

Question 6

The chart below lists the average increase in the annual car insurance rate based on the number of accidents a driver has.

Average Number of Accidents	Average Price Increase
1	19
2	39
3	59
4	79
5	99
6	119

If x represents the number of accidents a driver has, and y represents the average price increase which equation best represents the relationship of these two variables?

A. $y = 19x$

B. $y = 20x - 1$

C. $y = x^2$

D. $y = 3^{x-9}$

Your Notes

Hint: Use substitution to choose the equation that proves true for all data pairs.

Question 7

What is the value of y for the graph shown below when x = 2?

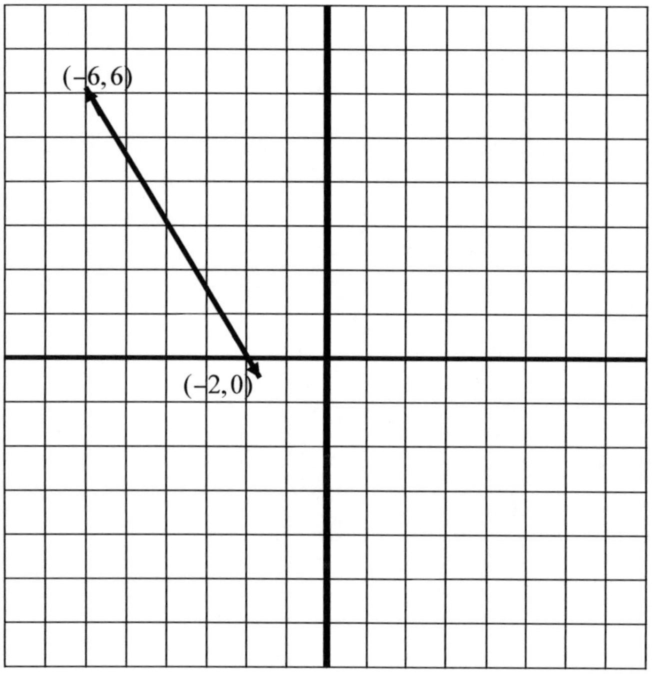

A. y = 0

B. y = 6

C. y = 3

D. y = -6

Your Notes

Hint: Extend the line of the graph to intersect the line x = 2.

Question 8

Jamie exercises every Monday afternoon. She jogs for exactly 2 miles at various speeds. She begins by speed walking for ½ a mile. Then she increases her speed and runs for quarter of a mile. Then she speed walks once again for a fifth of a mile. She walks the rest of her two miles at her normal walking speed. Which graph best represents this scenario?

A.

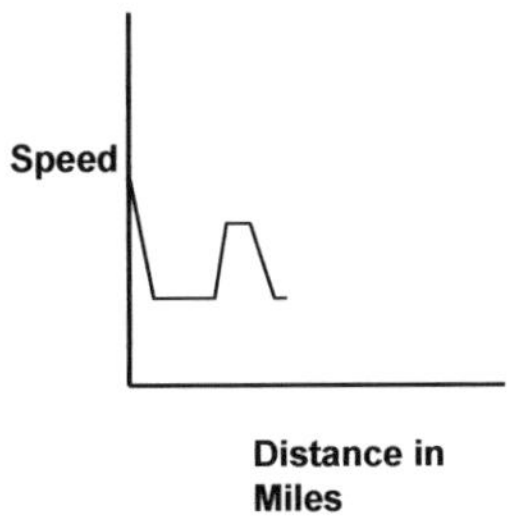

B.

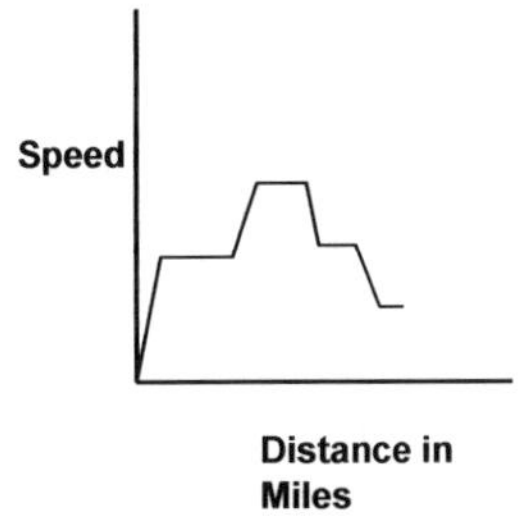

C.

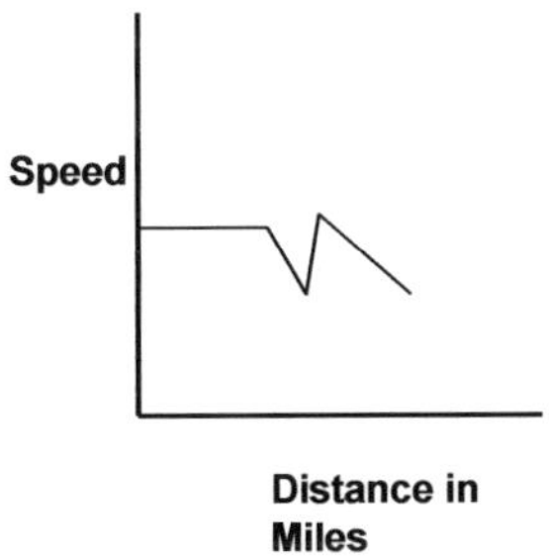

D.

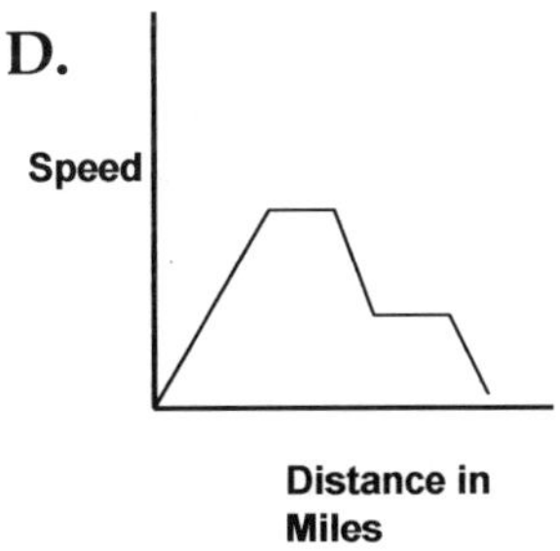

Your Notes

Hint: Determine whether an increase in speed would make the graph go up or down. Pay attention to the

Answers and Explanations for Objective 1

1. C is the correct answer choice. The independent value of 0 appears more than once.

2. B is the correct answer the equation x=-2, yields a vertical line, which is not a function.

3. A is the correct answer. The number of days is used to determine the cost of renting the video.

4. D is the correct answer. The graph is a parabola, which means the function is quadratic. This also implies that the x must be squared. The parabola is turned down which means that the coefficient of the squared term is negative. Its y-intercept is positive one; therefore the constant is plus one.

5. D is the correct answer choice. The inequality shown is a solid line and the graph is shaded below the line, therefore the function is "less than or equal to". The line also has a slope of 2 and a y-intercept of 1.

6. D is the correct answer, because the equation proves true for each data set.

7. D is the correct answer. Using the apparent slope of the line is $-3/2$, you can continue the line until you intersect the point where the x coordinate is 2 and you can then determine the coordinate y-value.

8. B is the correct answer. The problem implies that Jamie performs each exercise at a constant speed. However, her transition from one exercise to the next requires a ramp up or down in her speed.

Objective 2: Properties and Attributes of Functions

Question 1

Which of the following is the parent function for a linear equation?

A. $y = 1$

B. $y = x^2$

C. $y = |x|$

D. $y = x$

Your Notes

Hint: The exponent on the independent variable is 1 for linear functions.

Question 2

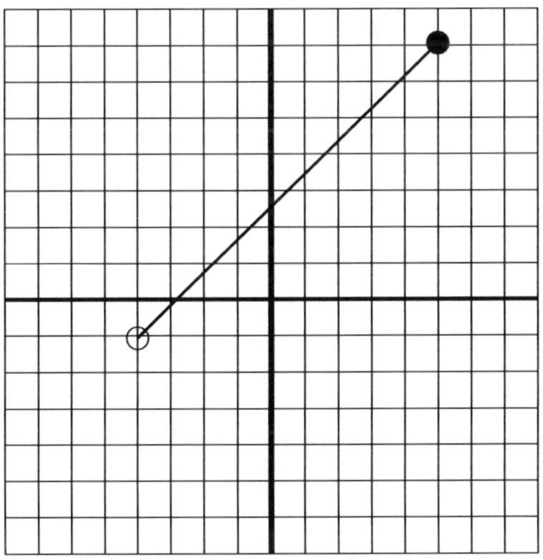

What is the range of the function shown above?

A. $-1 > y \geq 7$

B. $-1 \leq y < 7$

C. $-1 < y \leq 7$

Hint: The range represents all the valid dependent (i.e. y) values.

Question 3

Mary works at an umbrella store and she notices an the number of umbrellas sold is highest on rainy days. Mary plans to create a scatter plot comparing the number of rainy days to the number of umbrella's sold at her store. What type of correlation is most likely to form from the data set?

A. Positive Correlation

B. Negative Correlation

C. No Correlation

D. Undefined Correlation

Question 4

Which algebraic expression best relates the numbers in the sequence?

1, 10, 25, 46, 73...

A. $3n - 2n^2$

B. $2n^2 - 3n$

C. $3n^2 - 2$

D. $n^3 - 2n$

Your Notes

Hint: Use trial and error. The value of n is the position of a number in the sequence. To get the first number in the sequence use n=1. For the second, use n=2, and so on.

Question 5

Simplify the following expression. $-3(x-2)(x+3)+7x$

A. $3x^2 - 4x + 13$

B. $-3x^2 + 4x + 15$

C. $-3x^2 - 3x + 18$

D. $-3x^2 + 4x + 18$

Your Notes

Hint: Be sure to follow the order of operations.

Question 6

Dana's savings account is four times greater this month than it was last month. Yesterday she went shopping and spent \$15.00 from her savings account. If **c** represents the amount of money Dana had in her savings account last month, which expression best describes the amount of money in her account after shopping yesterday?

A. $4c - 15$

B. $4c + 15$

C. $(c + 4) - 15$

D. $\frac{1}{4}c - 15$

Hint: Decide what operation is implied by the words "greater" and "times".

Answers and Explanations for Objective 2

1. The correct answer is D. The parent function for a linear equation is y = x.

2. The correct answer is C, because the minimum y value is near negative one and the maximum y value is seven. The lower end of the range is not equal to -1 because there in an open circle at y = -1 in the graph.

3. The correct answer is A. The more it rains the more umbrellas Mary's store will probably sell. Because the variables move in the same direction there is a positive correlation.

4. The correct answer is C. Notice that the number in the third position of the sequence is twenty five and when you plug the number three into the correct equation the result is twenty five.

5. The correct answer is D.

$$-3(x-2)(x+3)+7x$$
$$(-3x+6)(x+3)+7x$$
$$-3x^2-9x+6x+18+7x$$
$$-3x^2+4x+18$$

6. The correct answer is A. Four times, means to multiply by four. Spending \$15 implies that amount subtracted from this month's savings account.

Objective 3: Linear Functions

Question 1

Which of the following describes the linear function shown below?

x	y
-5	-5.5
-4	-5
-2	-4
0	-3
2	-2
4	-1
6	0

A. $y = -2x - 3$

B. $y = \frac{1}{2}x - 3$

C. $y = -\frac{1}{2}x + 3$

D. $y = 2x - 3$

Your Notes

Hint: Use substitution, or derive the equation using coordinate pairs.

Question 2

Identify the slope of the line shown below.

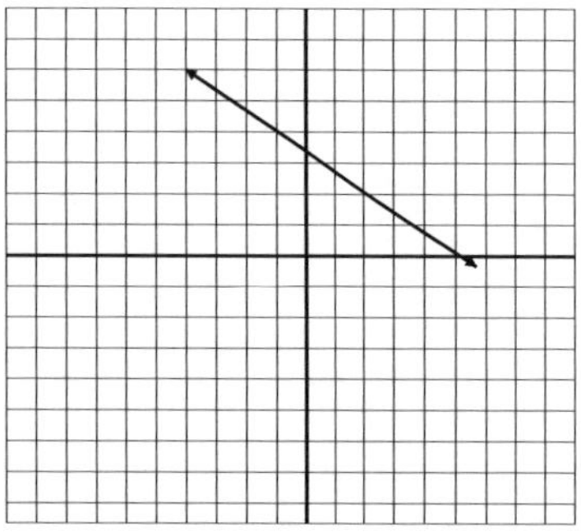

A. $m = \frac{2}{3}$

B. $m = -\frac{3}{2}$

C. $m = -\frac{2}{3}$

D. $m = \frac{3}{2}$

Question 3

If the slope of the line shown below is halved, which of the following could represent the equation of the new line?

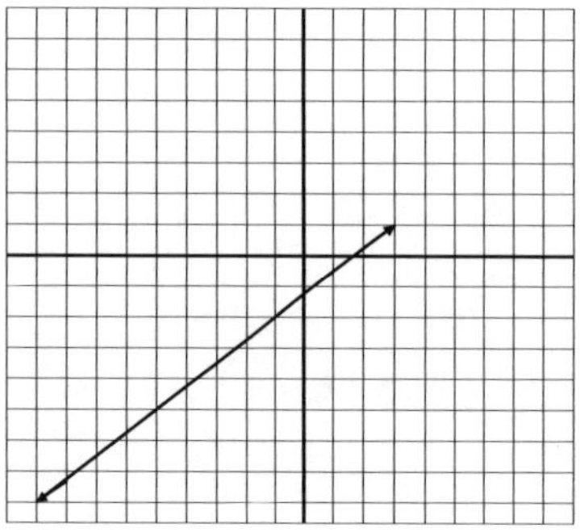

A. $y = 3/8x - 5/4$

B. $y = 1/4x - 1$

C. $y = 3/4x - 5/4$

D. $y = 3/2x - 5/4$

Your Notes

Hint:

Hint: Halved means divide by two.

Also, determine rise and run by counting grids in the figure.

Question 4

Tonya works every Friday at a new restaurant named Dailia's. Each Friday she works 6-hour shifts for $7.50 an hour, plus tips. Tonya is only allowed to keep 85% of the total amount of tip money she collects. If x represents the total amount of money she collects in tips which equation best describes, y, the amount of money Tonya makes each Friday?

A. $y = .85x + 7.50$

B. $y = 7.50x + 85$

C. $y = .85x + 45$

D. $y = 45x + .85$

Your Notes

Hint: Determine the rate of change and constant for the situation.

Question 5

The equation of $y = 1/3x - 2$ was changed to $y = 2x - 2$. Which of the following best describes the change in its graph?

A. The graph of $y = 1/3x - 2$ is steeper than the graph of $y = 2x - 2$.

B. The graph of $y = 1/3x - 2$ has a greater x-intercept than the graph of $y = 2x - 2$.

C. The graph of $y = 1/3x - 2$ is $1\frac{2}{3}$ units higher than the graph of $y = 2x - 2$.

D. The graph of $y = 1/3x - 2$ is $1\frac{2}{3}$ units lower than the graph of $y = 2x - 2$.

Hint: First determine which part of the equation was changed. (Slope or y-intercept)

Question 6

Which of the following best describes the relationship between The two lines shown below?

$$3x - 9y = -18$$
$$y = -3x - 2$$

A. The two lines are parallel

B. The two lines have the same y-intercept

C. The two lines are perpendicular

D. The two lines have the same x-intercept

Your Notes

Hint: Write both lines in slope-intercept form, and then compare the two equations.

Question 7

Which is the equation of the line that contains the points $(-9, 2)$ and $(3, 5)$?

A. $y = \frac{1}{4}x + \frac{17}{4}$

B. $y = \frac{1}{4}x - \frac{1}{4}$

C. $y = \frac{1}{4}x - \frac{17}{2}$

D. $y = -\frac{1}{4}x - 2$

Hint: First find the slope of the line, by using the slope formula. Then use substitution to solve for the y-intercept.

Question 8

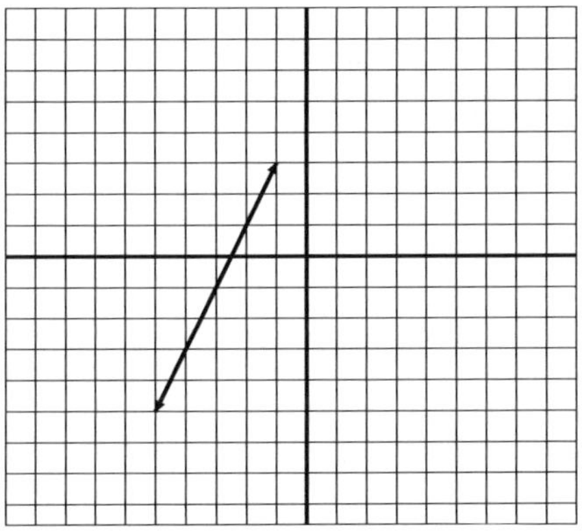

Which of the following is parallel to the line graphed above?

A. $y = -2x + 1$

B. $y = \frac{1}{2}x - 2$

C. $y = 2x$

D. $y = -\frac{1}{2}x + 1$

Question 9

Jimmy wrote the following expression to represent the amount of money he earns each week $y = .25x - 150$. Which of the following best represents a reasonable scenario for Jimmy?

A. Jimmy makes $25 an hour, but he has to pay $150 for cab fair in order to get to work.

B. Jimmy is salesman and earns 25% commission on all sales. He also earns a weekly salary of $150.

C. Jimmy owns a carwash. He keeps one-fourth of the weekly revenue minus $150 for next week's supplies.

D. None of the above

Your Notes

Hint: Parallel lines have the same slope.

Hint: The slope of the line is the income rate. Also, determine whether the constant amount should be deducted or added

Answers and Explanations for Objective 3

1. The correct answer is B. For example: slope of line $= \frac{-4 - -3}{-2 - 0} = \frac{-1}{-2} = \frac{1}{2}$.

2. The correct answer choice is C. Select two points from the graph and count the rise and run between the two points. Note negative and positive directions when you count.

3. The correct answer choice is A. The original slope is $\frac{3}{4}$. Half of three-fourths is $\frac{3}{8}$.

4. The correct answer choice is C. The rate of change for Tonya's situation is 85%. The constant for this situation is 6 hours * $7.50 per hour = $45.

5. The correct answer choice is B. The x-intercept of $y = \frac{1}{3}x - 2$ is 6, whereas the x intercept of $y = 2x - 2$ is 2. Find the x-intercept by setting y to 0 and solving for x.

6. The correct answer choice is C. Perpendicular slopes are negative reciprocals. The slope of the first line is positive one-third, and the slope of the second line is negative three.

7. The correct answer choice is A.

$$5 = \frac{1}{4}(3) + \frac{17}{4}$$

8. The correct answer is C. The original line has a slope of positive two. Parallel lines have the same slope.

9. The correct answer is C. The rate of change is .25, which can be expressed as the fraction $\frac{1}{4}$. Also answer C indicates that the operation on $150 is subtraction.

Objective 4: Linear Equations and Inequalities

Question 1

Jamie has $4.75 to spend at Smacker's Candy Store. Each lollipop is $0.25 plus tax and each candy bar is $0.75 plus tax. If x represents the number of lollipops and y represents the number of candy bars, which expression best represents a reasonable combination for Jamie to buy?

A. $.25x + .75y > \$4.75$

B. $.75y - .25x \geq \$4.75$

C. $.25x + .75y < \$4.75$

D. $.25y + .75x \leq \$4.75$

Question 2

Mela has been offered a position at two different restaurants in downtown Houston. Florita's Grill is willing to pay Mela $7.25 an hour plus 25% of her total tips. Rubey-Will's is willing to pay $6.00 an hour plus half of her total tip money. Meagan only wants to work 5 hours per shift. How much does she need to collect in tips in order to make the same amount of money, at either restaurant?

A. $25.00

B. $32.00

C. $16.00

D. $48.00

Your Notes

Hint: Determine whether the amount of money she spends has to be less than or greater than $4.75.

Hint: Set up a system of equations or use substitution.

Question 3

Which of the following is a solution to the inequality shown below?

$$-x + 3y < 8$$

A. (-5, 1) **B.** (-2, 4)

C. (7, 7) **D.** (6, 2)

Your Notes

Hint: Use substitution.

Question 4

The width of a rectangle is 2 inches shorter than its length. The perimeter of the rectangle is 28 inches. What is the width of the rectangle?

A. 8 **B.** 6

C. 10 **D.** 4

Hint: Set up a system of equations.

Question 5

Which of the following represents the complete set of solutions for the system of equations listed below?

$$16x - 8y = -32$$
$$2y = 4x + 8$$

A. $(-5, -6)$

B. There are no solutions

C. $(0, 4)$

D. There are an infinite number of solutions

Your Notes

Hint: Try the given points. Also, write both equations in the same form (e.g. slope–intercept form) and compare.

Answers and Explanations for Objective 4

1. The correct answer choice is C. Each x times twenty-five cents is the money spent on lollipops and y times seventy five cents is the money spent on candy bars. Since tax is also due, her total must be less than $4.75.

2. The correct answer choice is A. Both job's pay can be represented by two separate linear equations. The y-intercepts of the equations will be the result of 5 hours times the rate of pay. The slopes are the rate for which she retains her tips. The next step would be to set the two equations equal to each other, then solve for the independent variable.

3. The correct answer is D.

$$-6+3(2)<8$$
$$-6+6<8$$
$$0<8$$

4. The correct answer choice is B. The system of equations that you solve should look similar to the following:

$$W=L-2$$
$$2L+2W=28$$

5. The correct answer is D. When both equations are simplified you will find that they are identical. Since the solutions are where the lines intersect, and the lines actually overlay (are the same line), then there are an infinite number of solutions.

(YOUR NOTES)

Objective 5: Quadratic and Other Nonlinear Functions

Question 1

Which of the following quadratic equations will produce the widest parábola?

A. $y = 2x^2 + x - 2$

B. $y = -3x^2 - x + 1$

C. $y = -x^2$

D. $y = \frac{1}{2}x^2 + 3$

Question 2

The graph of $y = x^2 - 2$ was translated two units up. Which equation best describes the new graph after the translation.

A. $y = x^2 - 4$

B. $y = x^2 + 4$

C. $y = x^2$

D. $y = x^2 + 2$

Your Notes

Hint: Recall that the x^2 term determines the relative width of the graph.

Hint: Recall that modifying the constant term causes translation of the y coordinate.

Question 3

The five in the equation shown below was changed to negative three. Which of the following describes one effect this change has on the graph of the function?

$$y = 2x^2 + 5x - 1$$

A. The parabola is inverted

B. The parabola is shifted down

C. The parabola is shifted to the left

D. The parabola is shifted to the right

Your Notes

Hint: Find the vertex for both cases and compare locations.

Question 4

What are the roots of the quadratic function shown below?

$$y + 8 = 2x^2$$

A. $\{-2, 2\}$

B. $\{6, -6\}$

C. $\{\sqrt{5}, 2\}$

D. $\{-8, -2\}$

Hint: Set y to 0 and solve for x.

Question 5

The base of a triangle is 2 inches shorter than its height. If the area of this triangle is 24, how long is the height of the triangle?

A. 8

B. 10

C. 6

D. 4

Question 6

For a ball tossed in the air, the graph below shows the relationship between the ball's height in feet above the ground and the time after the toss.

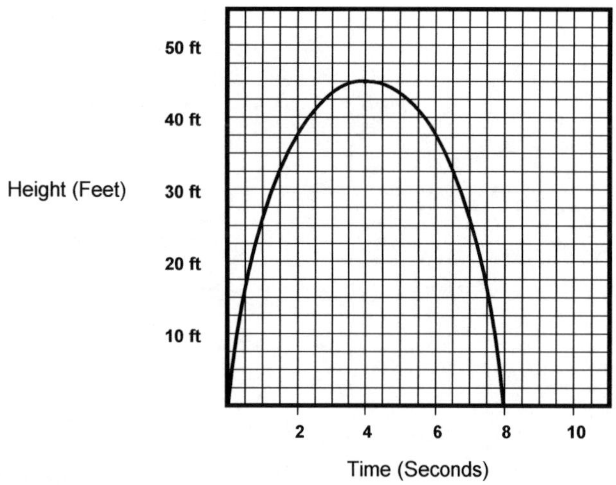

Which of the following is the best conclusion you can draw from the information given?

A. The maximum height the ball reached was greater than fifty-five feet.

B. The ball was above thirty feet for more than six seconds.

C. The ball was at its maximum height at four seconds after the throw.

D. The maximum height of the ball was forty feet.

Your Notes

Hint: Set up an equation for the area of the triangle, then factor to find the possible solutions.

Hint: Read each answer choice, carefully compare choices with the graph, and eliminate inaccurate choices.

Question 7

The area of a rectangle is $10x^3y^5$. If the width of rectangle is $2xy^7$, which expression best represents its length?

A. $5x^2y^2$

B. $\frac{5x^2}{y^2}$

C. $7x^4y^{12}$

D. $5x^3y^2$

Question 8

Simplify the following expression. $\frac{(2x^2y^3)^3}{(x^2y^3)(4x^{-2}y^8)}$

A. $\frac{3x^6}{2y^2}$

B. $\frac{2x^6}{y^2}$

C. $4x^4y^2$

D. $\frac{2y^2}{x^6}$

Your Notes

Hint: The area of a rectangle equals length times width.

Hint: Be sure to follow the order of operations.

Answers and Explanations for Objective 5

1. The correct answer choice is D. When a parabola is in standard form, the absolute value of the first term determines the width of the parabola. The smaller the value is, the wider the parabola.

2. The correct answer choice is C. When a parabola is in vertex form, the constant term determines the parabola's position along the y axis. Therefore, a change in its positive or negative change in it value will translate the parabola up or down. Since the graph was translated two units up the new value of the constant should be zero (i.e. -2+2=0).

3. The correct answer choice is D. When a parabola is expressed in standard form (i.e. $y = ax^2 + bx + c$), then the line of symmetry is found at $x = -b/2a$. In this case the line of symmetry shifts to the right when 5 is changed to 3, so the parabola shifts to the right.

4. The correct answer choice is A. One way to find the answer is by using the quadratic formula. $x=\frac{-b\pm\sqrt{b^2-4ac}}{2a}$

5. The correct answer choice is A. There are several methods for finding a solution. One of the more formal approaches is:

$$b=h-2$$

$$\frac{b\times h}{2}=24$$

$$\frac{(h-2)(h)}{2}=24$$

$$\frac{h^2-2h}{2}=24 \qquad h^2-2h=48$$

$$h^2-2h-48=0$$

$$(h-8)(h+6)=0$$

$$h=8 \quad h=-6$$

The height cannot be negative, so 8 is the correct solution.

Answers and Explanations for Objective 5 (Continued)

6. The correct answer choice is C. The vertex of the parabola represents the maximum height.

7. The correct answer choice is B. Divide the area by the length. Remember when dividing exponents subtract the powers.

8. The correct answer choice is B. Your solution should look similar to the following:

$$\frac{\left(2x^2y^3\right)^3}{\left(x^2y^3\right)\left(4x^{-2}y^8\right)}=\frac{8x^6y^9}{4y^{11}}=2x^6y^{-2}=\frac{2x^6}{y^2}$$

Question 1

Point A is 15 centimeters from the center of a circle with a diameter of 12 centimeters.

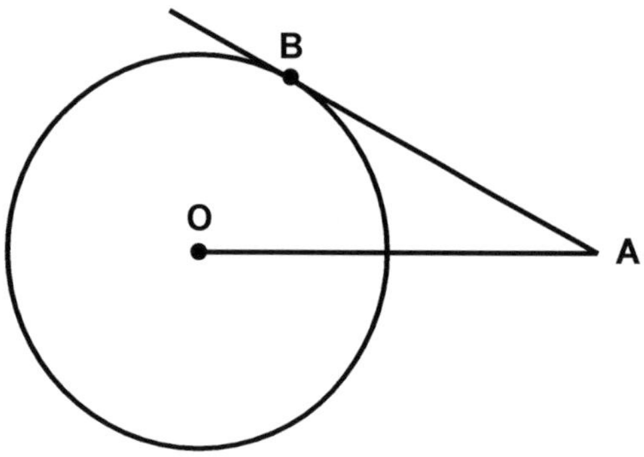

Find the length of the tangent $\overline{AB}$ drawn to circle O from point A.

A. 13.7 cm

B. 12.5 cm

C. 16.2 cm

D. 9 cm

Your Notes

Hint: Use the Pythagorean Theorem.

Question 2

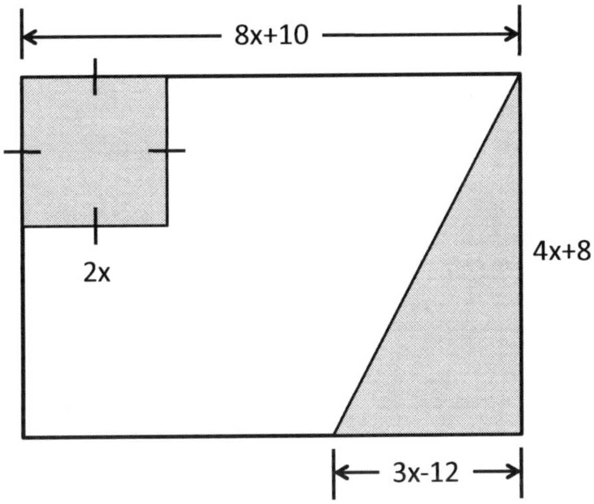

Which expression best represents the area of the un-shaded region?

A. $14x^2 - 78x - 168$

B. $22x^2 + 116x + 128$

C. $22x^2 + 92x + 32$

D. $14x^2 - 54x - 72$

Your Notes

Hint: Sum the shaded areas, then subtract for the area of the overall rectangle.

Question 3

Figure MNOP is translated so that O' is located at (-3, 2).

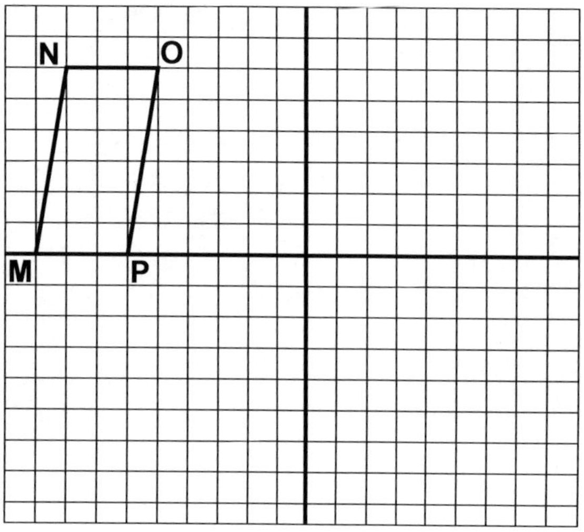

Which of the following represents the coordinates of M'?

A. (-7,-4)

B. (7, -4)

C. (-11, 4)

D. (-5, 3)

Your Notes

Hint: Determine the translation from **O** to .

Question 4

Which of the following describes the transformation from ABC to $A'B'C'$?

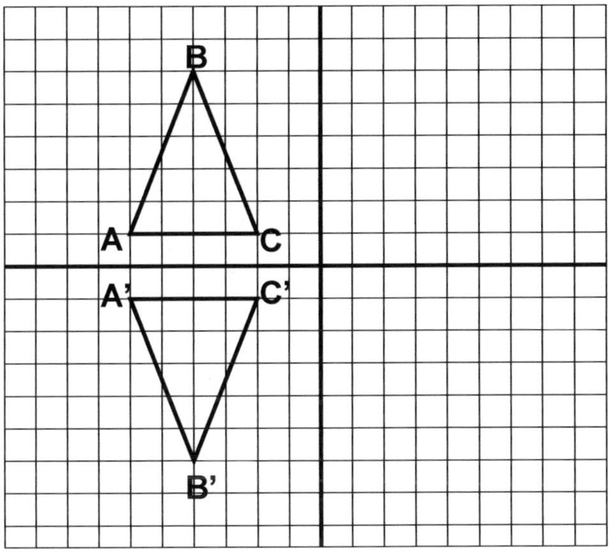

A. VABC was reflected across the y-axis to create triangleV$A'B'C'$.

B. VABC was reflected across the x-axis to create triangleV$A'B'C'$.

C. VABC was translated 2 units down to create triangleV$A'B'C'$.

D. VABC was translated 12 units down to create triangleV$A'B'C'$.

Your Notes

Hint: Determine whether or not there is a line of symmetry separating the two shapes.

Question 5

Which of the following is closest to the length of the diagonal for the rectangle shown below?

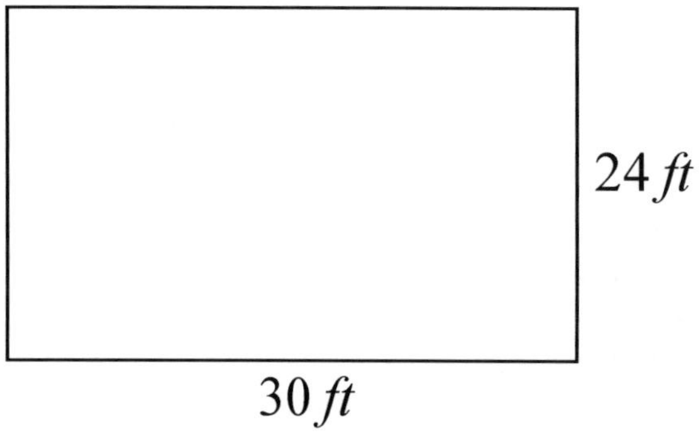

A. $6yds$

B. $18yds$

C. $12.8yds$

D. $38.4yds$

Question 6

The height of an equilateral triangle is 12 centimeters long. Which of the following is closest to the perimeter of this triangle?

A. $41.6cm$

B. $36cm$

C. $124.7cm$

D. $18cm$

Your Notes

Hint: Use Pythagorean's Theorem.

Hint: Use the rules for special right triangles to find the length of each side of the triangle.

Question 7

How long is side $\overline{AC}$ for the figure shown below?

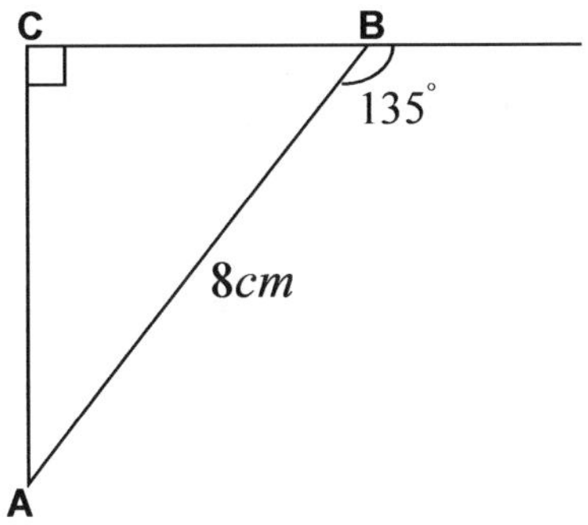

A. $4cm$

B. $8\sqrt{2}\,cm$

C. $6\sqrt{3}\,cm$

D. $4\sqrt{2}\,cm$

Your Notes

Hint: Use the rules for special right triangles.

Answers and Explanations for Objective 6

1. The correct answer choice is A. The radius of the circle must be perpendicular to the tangent line at B, forming the right triangle ΔOBA. With $\overline{OB} = 6\text{cm}$, Pythagorean's Theorem can be used to find the length of side $\overline{AB}$.

2. The correct answer choice is B. The first step is to find an expression for the area of the larger rectangle by multiplying (8x+10) by (4x+8). The total unshaded area should be found by subtracting the expressions for area of the square and triangle.

   Shaded Area $=(4x^2)+(6x^2-12x-48)=10x^2-12x-48$

   Unshaded Area $= (32x^2+104x+80)-(10x^2-12x-48)$
   $=22x^2+116x+128$

3. The correct answer choice is A. Point O was located at (-5, 6). The translation for the x coordinate is plus two. The translation for the y coordinate is minus four. Point M is located at (-9, 0). M′ is located at (-9+2, 0-4) = (-7, -4).

4. The correct answer choice is B. When a figure is reflected across the x-axis, the x coordinate remains the same while the y coordinate is multiplied by negative one.

5. The correct answer choice is C. The diagonal length of the rectangle is the hypotenuse of the right triangle with a base of 30ft and a height 24ft. Use the Pythagorean Theorem. Lastly, convert to yards by dividing the result by three. (Ouch! Yes, please be careful to note and track changes in all units.)

6. The correct answer choice is A. Given the sides are 12, the height of an equilateral triangle is found by the following operation:

   $$\frac{12}{\sqrt{3}} \times 2 = 13.8$$

   To find the perimeter multiply 13.8 times three.

7. The correct answer choice is D. The measure of angle ABC can be found by subtracting 135 from 180. The length of a leg of a 45 degree right triangle relates to the length of the hypotenuse by $\textit{hypotenuse} \div \sqrt{2}$; $8 \div \sqrt{2} = 4\sqrt{2}$.

Objective 7: Two- and Three-Dimensional Geometric Relationships and Shapes

Question 1

Which of the following has 5 faces, 8 edges, and 5 vertices?

A. Triangular Prism

B. Square Pyramid

C. Triangular Pyramid

D. Cube

Question 2

What is the surface area of the figure shown below?

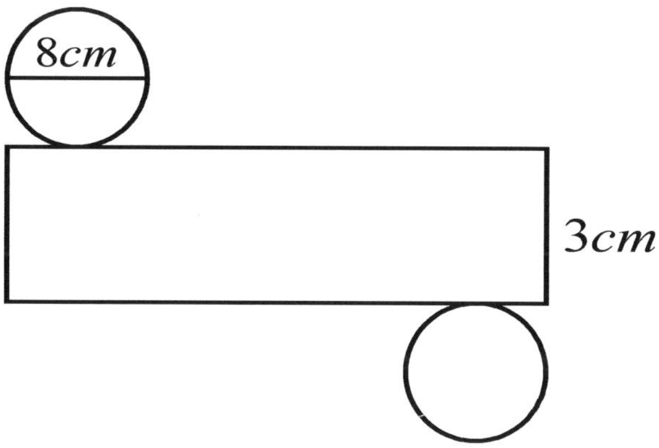

A. 36π

B. 176π

C. 56π

D. 256π

Your Notes

Hint: A vertex is a point where two or more lines meet and terminate. An edge is a line where two or more planes intersect. A face has two dimensions.

Hint: First determine what shape the net represents. Then use the appropriate surface area formula for that shape.

Question 3

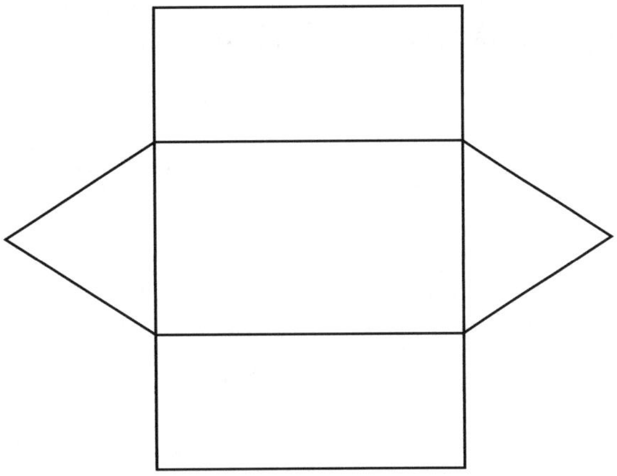

The net shown above represents which of the following three dimensional shapes?

A. Square Pyramid

B. Sphere

C. Triangular Prism

D. Triangular Pyramid

Your Notes

Hint: Mentally fold the net into a closed three-dimensional shape.

Select the name corresponding to the three dimensional figure that results from the folded net.

Question 4

The radius of a sphere with a volume of $2304\pi\, cm^3$ was made smaller. The new radius is $\frac{2}{3}$ of its original length. How much greater is the volume of the original sphere?

A. $2304\pi\ cm^3$

B. $1621\pi\ cm^3$

C. $2012\pi\ cm^3$

D. $1350\pi\ cm^3$

Hint: Find the new volume. Then find the difference between the two.

Question 5

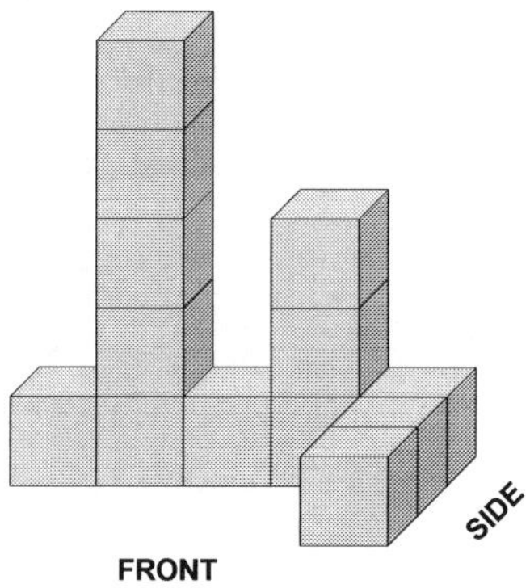

Which of the following represents the side view of the three dimensional figure shown above?

A. 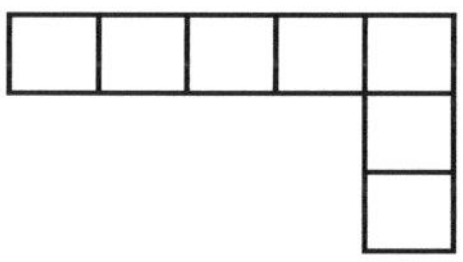

B. 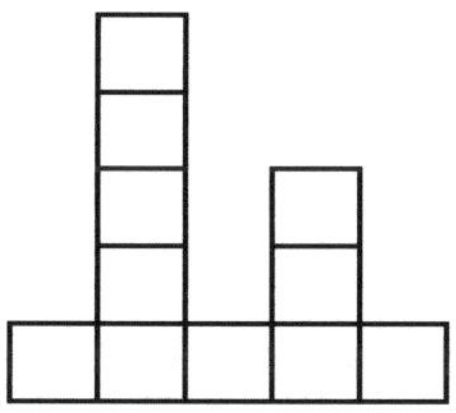

C. 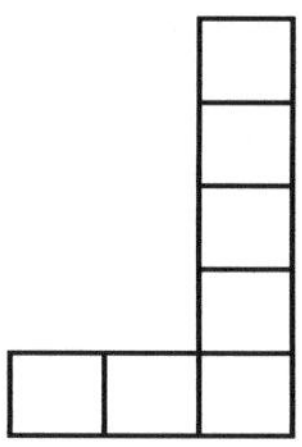

D. None of the above.

Your Notes

Hint: Visualize and determine which two dimensional figure represents the side view of the three dimensional figure.

Question 6

Which of the following sets of coordinates can be the vertices of an isosceles trapezoid?

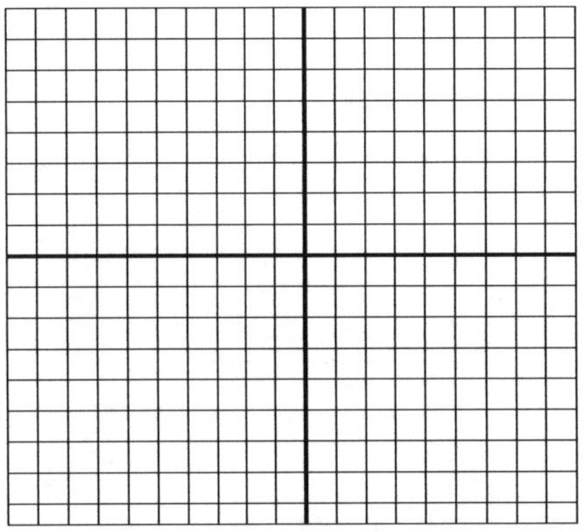

A. $(-6,4)(-8,0)(-3,4)(-1,0)$ **B.** $(-1,4)(0,6)(2,4)(3,6)$

C. $(-3,1)(-6,1)(-6,4)(-3,4)$ **D.** $(2,-4)(3,1)(5,1)(-1,-4)$

Your Notes

Hint: Plot the coordinates and sketch a figure to correspond to the points. Recall that an isosceles trapezoid has two congruent sides.

Question 7

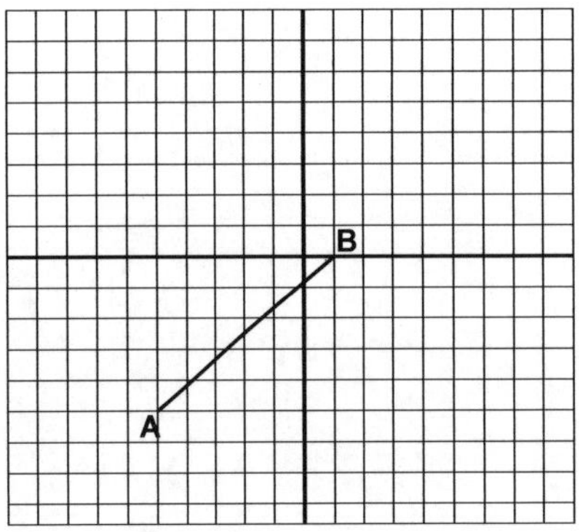

What is the best approximation of the length of the line segment $\overline{AB}$?

A. 7.8 units **B.** 6.4 units

C. 3.3 units **D.** 6.2 units

Hint: Use the distance formula.

Question 8

8. The line segment $\overline{AB}$ has a midpoint at point M. Point A is located at (-4, 5) and point M is located at (1,-3). What are the coordinates of point B?

A. (-6, 11) **B.** (-1.5, 1)

C. (-5, -11) **D.** (6,-11)

Your Notes

Hint: Use the midpoint formula.

Question 9

VABC is a right triangle.

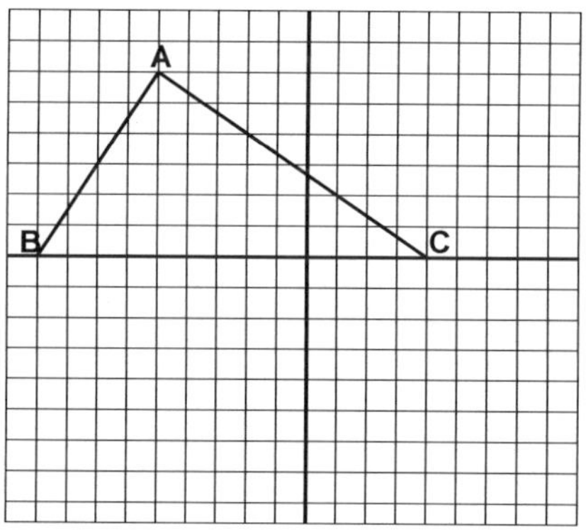

Which of the following pair of equations describes the lines of the right angle in VABC?

A. $y = \frac{3}{2}x - \frac{27}{2}$ *and* $y = -\frac{2}{3}x + \frac{8}{3}$

B. $y = -\frac{3}{2}x + \frac{27}{2}$ *and* $y = \frac{2}{3}x + \frac{8}{3}$

C. $y = 0$ *and* $y = -\frac{3}{2}x + \frac{27}{2}$

D. $y = \frac{3}{2}x + \frac{27}{2}$ *and* $y = -\frac{2}{3}x + \frac{8}{3}$

Hint: A right angle comprises perpendicular lines.

Answers and Explanations for Objective 7

1. The correct answer choice is B. A square pyramid has 5 faces, 8 edges, and 5 vertices.

2. The correct answer choice is C. The net shown represents a cylinder of radius 4 cm. The formula for the surface area of a cylinder is $2\pi rh+2\pi r^2$. Therefore S.A. = 2 x π x 4 x 3 + 2 x π x $(4)^2$ = 24π + 32π = 56π.

3. The correct answer choice is letter C. A triangular prism has three rectangular faces and two triangular faces.

4. The correct answer choice is letter B. The scale factor is $\left(\frac{2}{3}\right)^3 = \frac{8}{27}$. Multiply the original volume by the scale factor and subtract the new volume from the old.

5. The correct answer choice is answer C. The side view of the three dimensional shape is appears two dimensional, with a width of 3 units and a height of five units.

6. The correct answer choice is A. An isosceles trapezoid has two parallel sides and two congruent sides as depicted below.

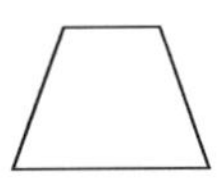

7. The correct answer choice is A. The distance formula is used to provide the length of a line segment when given the segments two endpoints. The coordinates of point A are (-5, -5) and the coordinates of point B are (1, 0).

$$d=\sqrt{(x_2 - x_1)+(y_2 - y_1)}$$

$$d=\sqrt{(1--5)^2+(0--5)^2}$$

$$d=\sqrt{61}$$

$$d=7.8$$

Answers and Explanations for Objective 7 (Continued)

8. The correct answer choice is D. Use the midpoint formula. Plug in all the values you know and solve for the missing endpoint.

$$\text{Midpoint}=\left(\frac{x_1+x_2}{2},\frac{y_1+y_2}{2}\right)$$

$$1=\frac{-4+x}{2} \qquad 2=-4+x \qquad 6=x$$

$$-3=\frac{5+y}{2} \qquad -6=5+y \quad -11=y$$

(6,-11)

9. The correct answer choice is D. The equation of the line for side $\overline{\mathbf{AC}}$ is $y=\frac{3}{2}x+\frac{27}{2}$, and the equation of the line for side $\overline{\mathbf{AB}}$ is $y=-\frac{2}{3}x+\frac{8}{3}$.

Objective 8: Measurement and Similarity

Question 1

Which expression represents the area of the regular hexagon shown below?

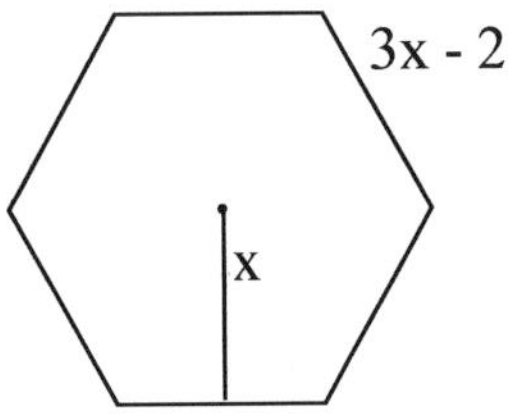

$$area = \frac{1}{2}(apothem)(perimeter)$$

A. $9x^2 - 6x$

B. $9x - 6$

C. $18x - 12x$

D. $15x^2$

Your Notes

Hint: The apothem extends from the center of a polygon to the midpoint of an edge.

Question 2

The circle shown below has a radius of 4.5 cm. The arc APB is $240°$. Find the area of the shaded sector.

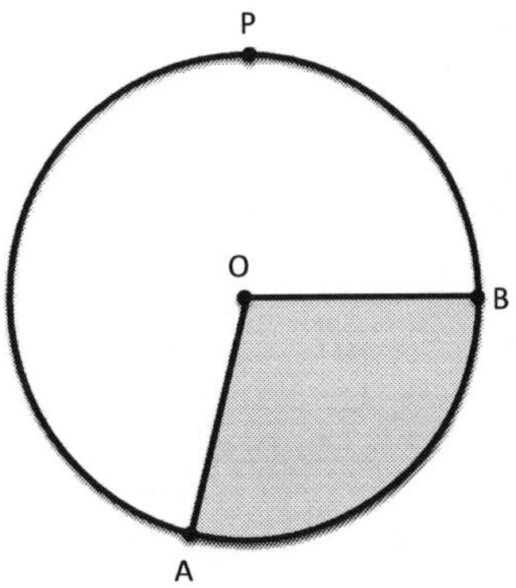

A. $42.41cm^2$

B. $21.21cm^2$

C. $18.85cm^2$

D. $9.42cm^2$

Hint: Set up a proportion.

Question 3

The diameter of the track at McNeil High School is 50 feet long. The picture below represents the track at the high school.

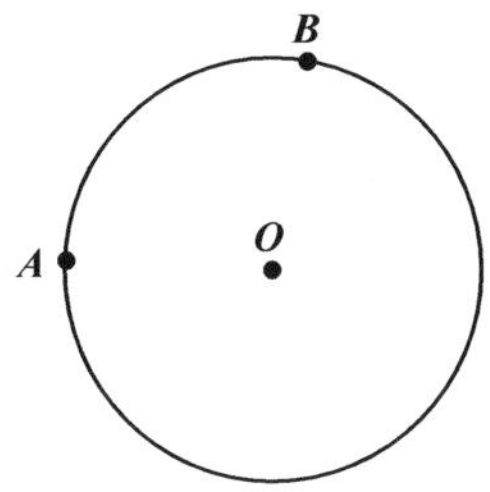

If Jimmy ran from point A to point B, and the measure of the corresponding central angle, $\angle AOB$, is 95°, approximately how many feet did Jimmy run?

A. $52.50\,ft$ **B.** $518.14\,ft$

C. $115.63\,ft$ **D.** $41.45\,ft$

Your Notes

Hint: Set up a proportion.

Question 4

Below is a picture of a uniformly-graduated cylindrical measuring cup that is partially filled with liquid, as shown, and that has a diameter of 8 inches and a height of 12 inches.

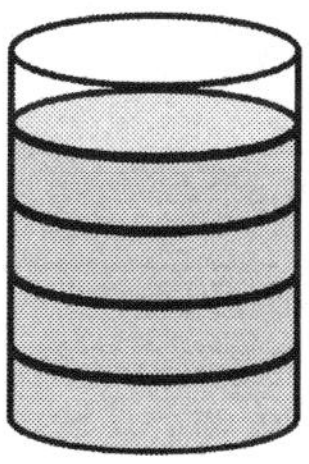

Which of the following is closet to the volume of the liquid inside the measuring cup?

A. $482.55\,in^3$ **B.** $603.19\,in^3$

C. $1930.19\,in^3$ **D.** $301.59\,in^3$

Hint: Determine the fraction of the measuring cup the liquid occupies. Determine the maximum volume of the cylinder. Then multiply.

Question 5

Which of the following sets of figures is not similar?

A.

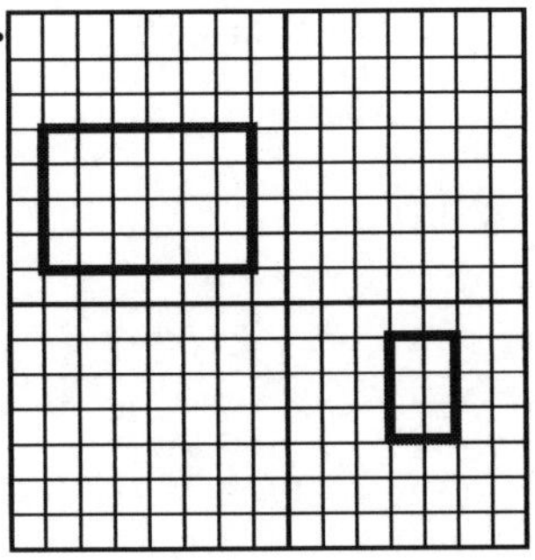

B.

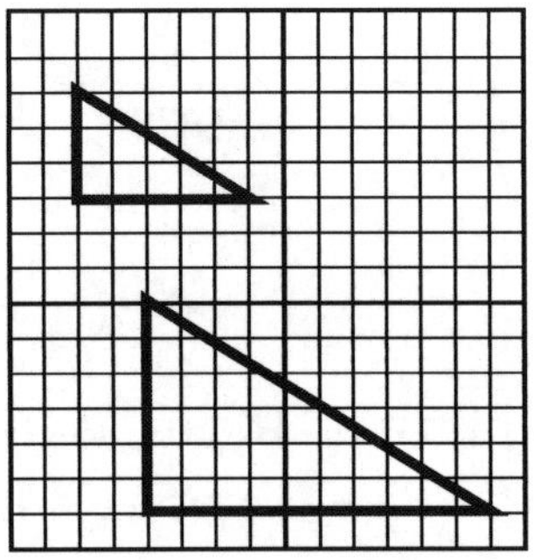

C.

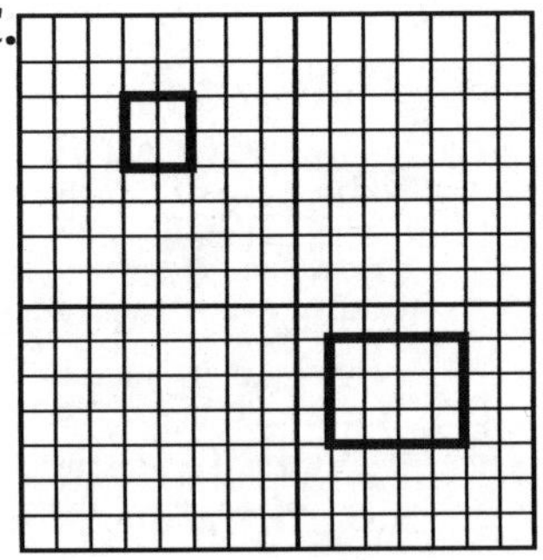

D.

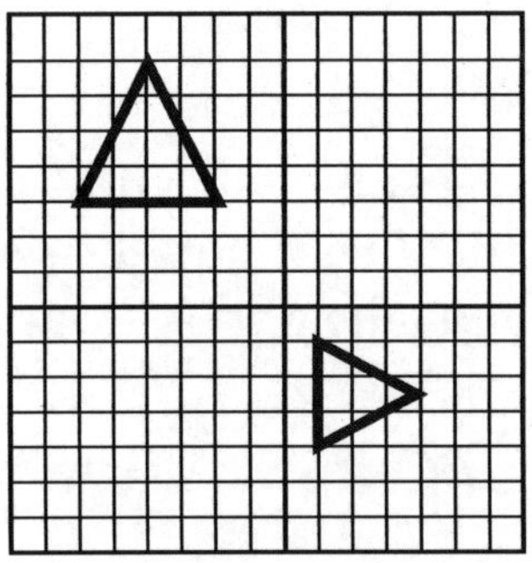

Your Notes

Hint: Similar polygons have proportional side lengths.

Question 6

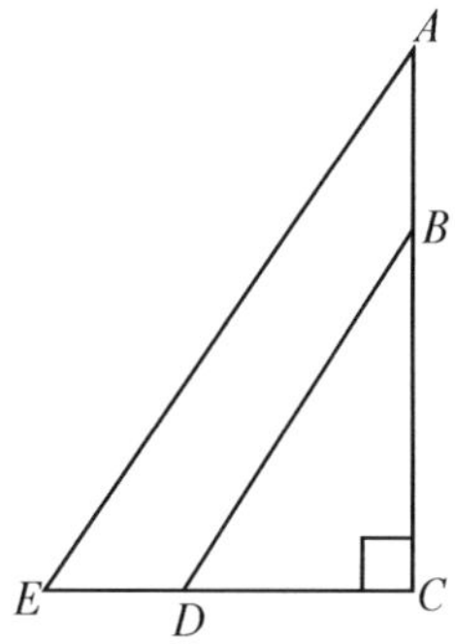

The length of side $\overline{EC}$ is 8 inches. The length of side $\overline{ED}$ is 3 inches. If the area of $VACE$ is 64 square inches and $VACE : VBCD$, what is the area of $VBCD$?

A. $15in^2$ **B.** $32in^2$

C. $40in^2$ **D.** $25in^2$

Hint: The ratio of the areas of similar figures is equal to the scale factor squared.

Question 7

A rectangular prism with an original volume of 48 cubic feet was made bigger. Each dimension was increased by a scale factor of 2.5. What is the volume of the new prism?

A. $360 ft^3$ **B.** $168 ft^3$

C. $750 ft^3$ **D.** $120 ft^3$

Your Notes

Hint: Recall that 2.5 is the scale factor for each dimension. The volumes are proportional to the scale factor

Question 8

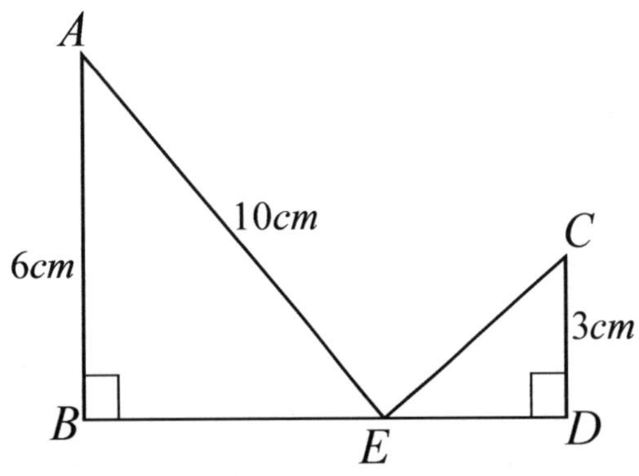

V*ABE* : V*CDE*

Based on the information presented above, how long is $\overline{ED}$?

A. 2*cm**B.** 4*cm*

C. 5*cm*

D. 7*cm*

Question 9

If the radius of a cone is changed by a scale factor of ½, which of The following is true for the surface area of the new cone?

A. The new surface area will be half the original surface area.

B. The new surface area will be one fourth the original surface area.

C. The new surface area will be the same as the original surface area.

D. Cannot be determined with the given information.

Your Notes

Hint: Set up a proportion.

Hint: If the scale factor of each dimension is one-half, determine the scale factor for the total surface area.

Answers and Explanations for Objective 8

1. The correct answer choice is A. The perimeter of the hexagon can be found by multiplying 3x-2 by six, because each of the six side length are congruent. Next, plug in the perimeter and the apothem into the formula.

$$\text{area}=\frac{1}{2}(\text{apothem})(\text{perimeter})$$

$$\text{area}=\frac{1}{2}(x)(18x-12)$$

$$\text{area}=9x^2-6x$$

2. The correct answer choice is B. The angle that corresponds to the shaded sector can be found by subtracting 240 from 360. The area of the shaded sector can be found by setting up a proportion.

$$\frac{\text{angle of shaded sector}}{360°}=\frac{\text{area of shaded sector}}{\text{total area}}$$

$$\frac{120°}{360°}=\frac{x}{63.6}$$

$$x=21.21\text{cm}^2$$

3. The correct answer choice D. The answer can be found by setting up a proportion.

$$\frac{\text{angle of arc}}{360°}=\frac{\text{length of arc}}{\text{circumference}}$$

$$\frac{95°}{360°}=\frac{x}{157}$$

4. The correct answer choice is A. Find the volume of the entire measuring cup, then multiply the total volume by $\frac{4}{5}$, because the liquid only occupies $\frac{4}{5}$ of the total volume.

5. The correct answer choice is C. The similar figures have the same shape, but different sizes. The smaller figure for answer choice C is a square and the larger figure is a rectangle.

Answers and Explanations for Objective 8 (Continued)

6. The correct answer choice is D. The base of VBCD is 5 inches. The scale factor is $\left(\frac{5}{8}\right)^2$. Multiply the area of VACE by the scale factor.

7. The correct answer choice is C. When each dimension is changed by a certain scale factor, the volume is changed by that scale factor cubed. Multiply the original volume by $(2.5)^3$.

8. The correct answer choice is B. The triangles are similar. $\overline{BE}$ is 8 inches by Pythagorean's Theorem. $\overline{DE}$ can be found by setting up a proportion.

$$\frac{6}{8}=\frac{3}{x}; \quad x=4$$

9. The correct answer choice is B. When each dimension is changed by a certain scale factor, the surface area is changed by that scale factor squared. ½ squared is ¼.

Objective 9: Percent, Proportionality, Probability, and Statistics

Question 1

A researcher is trying to figure out how large is the income gap between the highest paid attorney and the lowest paid cashier in a certain county. Which measure of central tendency would be the most helpful?

A. Mean　　**B.** Range

C. Mode　　**D.** Median

Your Notes

Hint: The mean is the average. The median is the middle number of an ordered set. The range is the highest number minus the smallest number. The mode is the number that appears the most.

Question 2

A spinner has five different color-coded sections. Each section has the same probability of occurring after a spin of the pointer. The colors are blue, green, pink, red, and black. In order to win $10,000, Neisha must roll a fair die and get an odd number. The spinner also has to land on either green or black. What is the probability that Neisha will win the money?

A. $\frac{5}{11}$　　**B.** $\frac{1}{15}$

C. $\frac{1}{5}$　　**D.** $\frac{1}{30}$

Hint: Multiply the individual (independent) probabilities.

Question 3

Mary, John, Jasmine, and Dana all contribute a specific amount of money for their senior trip. Altogether, they saved $492.00, if John contributed $36.00, and Mary contributed $72.00, what percent of the total did Jasmine and Dana contribute?

A. 22%   B. 78%

C. 14%   D. 69%

Your Notes

Hint: Find the amount that Dana and Jasmine contributed and convert it into a percent by setting up a proportion.

Question 4

A car that originally cost $10,580.00 is on sale for $ 9,220.00. What percent of the original price is the sale price?

A. 80%   **B.** 78%

C. 75%   **D.** 87%

Hint: Set up a proportion.

Question 5

Mary owes Johnny 15% of her check this week. Mary gave Johnny $48.00 to exactly clear her debt. How much was Mary's check?

A. $480 **B.** $289

C. $500 **D.** $320

Question 6

The circle chart shown below was created after a survey was taken that asked a group of 125 people which brand of soup they preferred. Which of the following best describes the data?

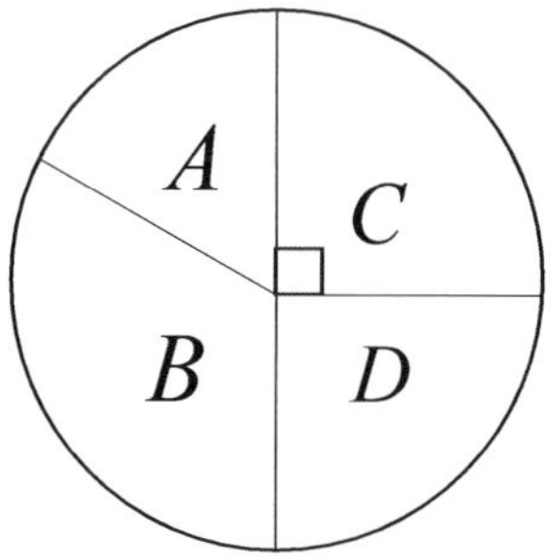

A. 25% of the people preferred Brand B.

B. About sixty two people preferred either Brand A or Brand C.

C. More than thirty people preferred Brand D.

D. More than 80 people preferred either Brand A or Brand B.

Your Notes

Hint: Set up a proportion.

Hint: Carefully determine which answer choice is supported by the figure.

Answers and Explanations for Objective 9

1. The correct answer choice is B. The Range is equal to the largest value minus the smallest value.

2. The correct answer choice is C. The probability of Neisha winning the $10,000 is a compound of independent events. First you should find the probability of her rolling an odd number on a die. The probability of her rolling an odd number is equal to 3/6 or 1/2. The probability of her spinning the colors green or black is equal to 2/5. To find probability of both of these outcomes happening together you should multiply the two probabilities.

3. The correct answer choice is B. First determine how much money Jasmine and Dana contributed by subtracting the amount Mary and John contributed from the total amount contributed. Next, solve a percentage ratio to find the solution.

$$\$492-(\$72+\$36)=\$384$$

$$\frac{\$382}{\$492}=\frac{x}{100}$$

4. The correct answer choice is D. A percentage ratio should be used for this problem.

$$\frac{\$9220}{\$10{,}580}=\frac{x}{100}$$

5. The correct answer choice is D. A percentage ratio should be used to solve this problem.

$$\frac{\$48}{\$x}=\frac{15}{100}$$

6. The correct answer choice is C. Based of the chart 25% of the people surveyed choose Brand D. 25% of 125 is 31.25 therefore, more than 30 people preferred Brand D.

Objective 10: Mathematical Processes and Tools Used in Problem Solving

Question 1

Mary has a bag of marbles that are all the same size, but of assorted colors. There are five green, two yellow, six blue, three red, and two black marbles. She drew from her bag of marbles ten times. The results of her drawings are shown below.

yellow	1
green	2
red	3
blue	3
black	1

Based on the information above which of the following are true?

A. The experimental and theoretical probability of drawing a red marble is the same.

B. The theoretical probability of drawing a green marble is less than the experimental.

C. The theoretical probability of drawing a black marble is more than the experimental.

D. The experimental probability of drawing a blue marble is $33\frac{1}{3}\%$.

Your Notes

Hint: Remember the experimental probability is what actually occurred, and the theoretical probability is what you expect to occur.

Question 2

A series of cubes are shown below.

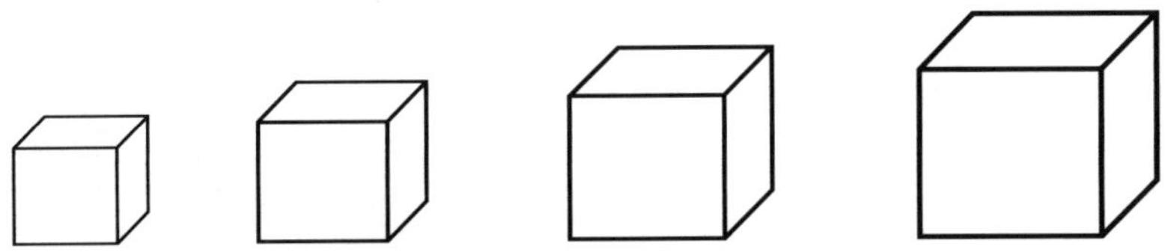

$SA = 6\text{ cm}^2$ $SA = 54\text{ cm}^2$ $SA = 486\text{ cm}^2$ $SA = 4374\text{ cm}^2$

If this pattern continues what will be the side length of the 10th cube?

Question 3

The center of the circle shown below is offset from the origin of the coordinate axes. Which of the following is closest to the area of the circle? (Assume that the grid spacing is 1 unit)

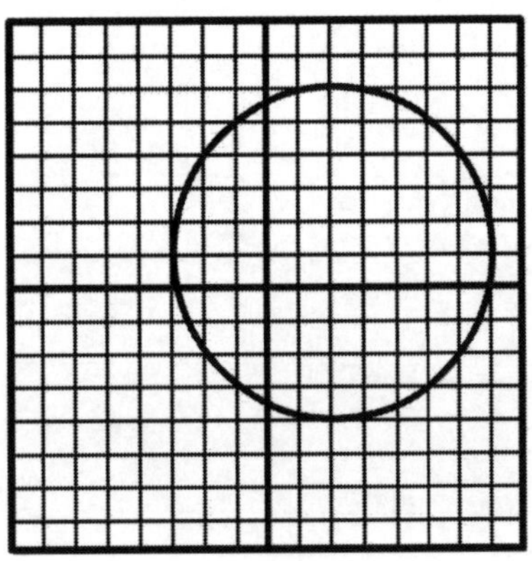

A. 34π

B. 36π

C. 25π

D. 6π

Your Notes

Hint: First determine the side lengths of each cube, then determine the pattern.

Hint:

Question 4

Mr. Ying is planning on building a new garden in his backyard. His current square garden has an area of 240.25 square feet. He plans on making his new garden twice as big, and changing the shape of the garden into a circle. Which of the following is closet to the diameter of the new garden?

A. 31 *feet* **B.** 24.8 *feet*

C. 60 *feet* **D.** 15.5 *feet*

Question 5

Monique's Bridal Boutique is having a store-wide sale. The bargain is "20% off the list price". Gigi is planning on buying a wedding dress during the sale and using a coupon for an additional 30% off the sale price. Which of the following expresses the amount Gigi will pay for a weeding dress that has a listed price of x dollars?

A. $C = .56x$ **B.** $C = .5x$

C. $C = .6x$ **D.** none of the above

Your Notes

Hint: First determine the area of the new garden.

Hint: A "20% off" sale means that the purchase price is 80% of the original price.

Answers and Explanations for Objective 10

1. The correct answer choice is C. The theoretical probability for drawing a black marble is 2 out of 18 or 11.1%. The experimental probability of drawing a black marble is 1 out of 10 or 10%.

2. The correct answer is 19,683 cm. The first step in solving this problem is to determine a pattern in the series of cubes. The formula to find the surface area of a cube is $SA = 6s^2$. After solving for the side lengths for each cube, the pattern becomes evident – the side length increases by a factor of 3, or the SA increases by a factor of 9. FYI, a sequence that increases by a constant factor is called a geometric sequence (but don't get hung up on the name).

   The next step is to find the pattern between the cubes. The first cube has a side length of 1 cm, the 2nd has a side length of 3 cm, the 3rd has a side length of 9 cm, and the 4th has a side length of 27 cm. Therefore, every cube has a side length three times as great as the previous cubes side length. If the pattern continues the 10th cube will have a side length of 19,683 cm.

3. The correct answer choice is C. The formula to find the area of a circle is πr^2. The first step in answering this question is to find the radius of the circle. It can be found by finding the distance from the center of the circle to the outside edge of the circle. By symmetry the radius is 5.

4. The correct answer choice is B. The problem states that the new area will be twice as big as the previous area, therefore it can be found by multiplying 240.25 by two. Next, we can find the diameter by using the area of the new circular garden.

5. The correct answer is A. The percentage of full price that represents the purchase price at 20% off can be found by subtracting 20% from 100%. Next, the percentage of the sale price that Gigi will pay after applying her coupon can be found by subtracting 30% from 100%. Multiply these two values to find the percentage of the full price that Gigi will pay, i.e.:

$$80\% \times 70\% = 0.8 \times 0.7 = 0.56$$

CHAPTER 5

PRACTICE AND PERFORMANCE

TEST 1

- NO TIME LIMIT -

Question 1

Below is a diagram of Jimmy's neighborhood.

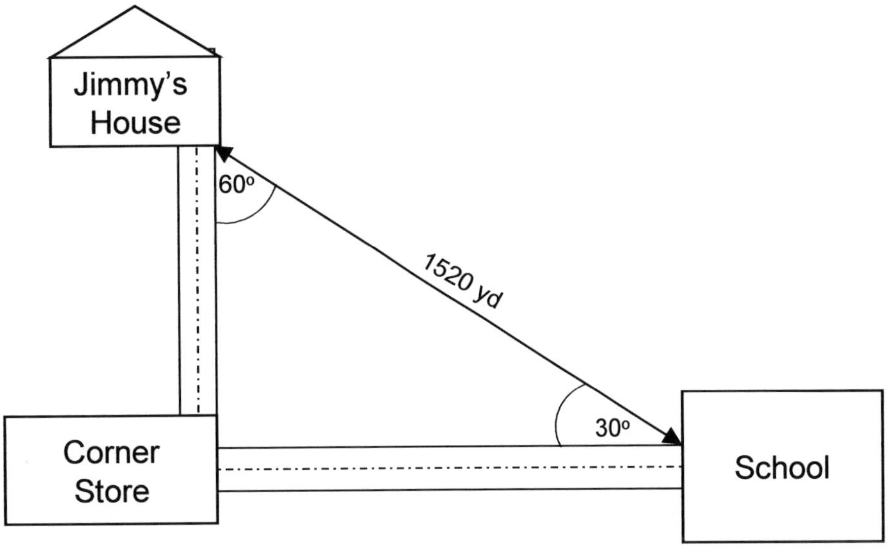

The diagonal distance from Jimmy's house to his school is 1,520 yards long. If Jimmy walks from his house to the store, then walks to school about how far will Jimmy have to walk?

A. 1.7*miles* **B.** .88*miles*

C. 2.2*miles* **D.** 1.2*miles*

Your Notes

Question 2

If the graph of $y = 2x^2 + 3$ is changed to $y = \frac{1}{2}x^2 + 1$, which of the following will occur?

A. The graph will shift two units down, and become narrower

B. The graph will shift two units down, and become wider

C. The graph will shift two units up, and become wider

D. The graph will shift two units up, and become narrower

Question 3

Tyrica bought two t-shirts and three pairs of jeans. The cost of each shirt was $9.99, and the cost of each pair of jeans was $13.99. Tyrica has a coupon for 15% off her total purchase. Which equation could be used to find the price of the clothing with the coupon before taxes?

A. $\left[(9.99 \times 2) + (13.99 \times 3)\right] \times 15\%$

B. $(13.99 \times 3) + (9.99 \times 2) + 15\%$

C. $\left[(9.99 \times 3) + (13.99 \times 2)\right] \times 85\%$

D. $\left[(9.99 \times 2) + (13.99 \times 3)\right] \times 85\%$

Your Notes

Question 4

A pie graph was created based on the following chart.

Favorite Colors	
Blue	36
Green	41
Red	46
Pink	39

What central angle should be used for the section labeled green?

A. 91.1° **B.** 86.7°

C. 25° **D.** 41°

Question 5

The hypotenuse of the right triangle, $VABC$, is side $\overline{AC}$ and it is 15 inches long. If side $\overline{AB}$ and $\overline{BC}$ are perpendicular and side $\overline{AB}$ is 9 inches long, what is the area of $VABC$?

A. $12 inches$ **B.** $36 inches$

C. $67.5 inches$ **D.** $54 inches$

Your Notes

Question 6

The slope of a line is 2, and it passes through the origin. Which of the following lines is parallel to this line?

A. $4x + 2y = 10$

B. $-2x + 4y = 6$

C. $-2y = -4x$

D. $2y = 4x + 1$

Question 7

BigBuck Movie Rental charges a base fee of $2.00 plus $.75 per day the movie is rented. If Mary wants to find, c, the cost of renting a movie for, x, amount of days, which of the following equations should she use?

A. $2.00x + .75 = c$

B. $.75(2.00 + x) = c$

C. $.75x + 2.00 = c$

D. $2.00 - .75x = c$

Question 8

Jerry makes $15.00 per adult and $12.00 per child every time he cuts a person's hair. Which of the following is needed to determine the amount of money Jerry makes in a given period of time?

A. The age of the person getting their hair cut

B. The amount of hours he works

C. The number of adults getting their hair cut and the total number of people getting their hair cut

D. The number of children getting their hair cut and the total number of hours he worked

Question 9

How many ice cubes can be made from a block of ice with the Dimensions 14 cm by 12 cm by 13 cm, if each ice cube has a side length of 2 cm?

A. 195

B. 364

C. 273

D. 546

Your Notes

Question 10

Your Notes

Below is a table that illustrates the relationship between the age of a person and their average salary per week.

age	wage per week
(18-20)	$300
(21-23)	$425
(30-32)	$800

Based on the information above, how much money would a 37 year old person make per week?

A. \$1,050

B. \$1,425

C. \$2,000

D. \$1,675

Question 11

Meagan has piece of cloth with a rectangular shape that has a Perimeter of 100 inches and a width of 20 inches. If Meagan cuts part of the cloth to make a square napkin with side length 10 inches, about how much cloth area will she have left?

A. $500\,in^2$

B. $900\,in^2$

C. $1000\,in^2$

D. $1900\,in^2$

Question 12

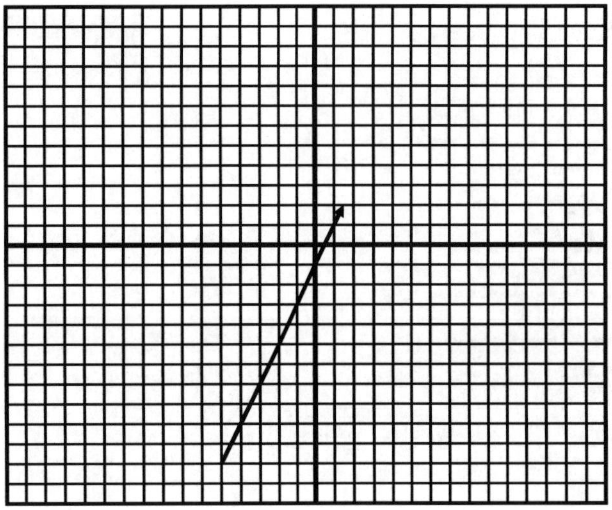

What is the equation of this line?

A. $y = -2x - 1$

B. $y = -\frac{1}{2}x - 1$

C. $y = \frac{1}{2}x - 1$

D. $y = 2x - 1$

Your Notes

Question 13

Which of the following statements are true, if line m and n are parallel?

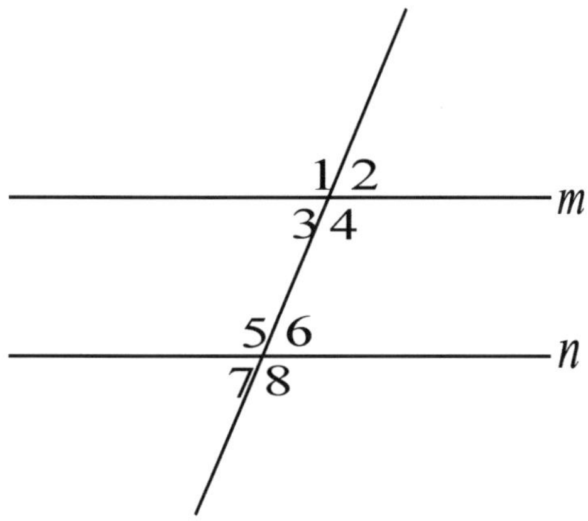

A. $\angle 4 \text{ and } \angle 6$ are supplementary angles

B. $\angle 5 \text{ and } \angle 2$ are congruent angles

C. $\angle 6 \text{ and } \angle 7$ are supplementary angles

D. $\angle 1 \text{ and } \angle 3$ are complementary angles

Your Notes

Question 14

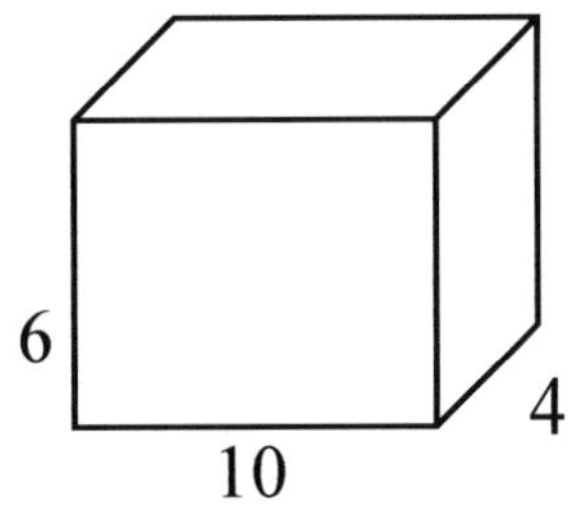

Which of the following are similar to the figure shown above?

A. 8 by 12 by 15

B. 12 by 8 by 20

C. 12 by 20 by 10

D. 6 by 10 by 5

Question 15

Which of the following is not be a point represented by the graph, $5x - 2y \le 12$?

A. (2, –12)

B. (–2, –5)

C. (2,6)

D. (–2, –3)

Your Notes

Question 16

What is the value of x when the line $3x + 2y = 9$, crosses the x-axis?

A. $\frac{2}{3}$

B. $-\frac{3}{2}$

C. $\frac{9}{2}$

D. 3

Question 17

The price of gasoline rapidly increased before it finally levels off and remained constant for a period of time. Then it rapidly decreased before it once again leveled off and remained constant. Which graph depicts this situation?

A.
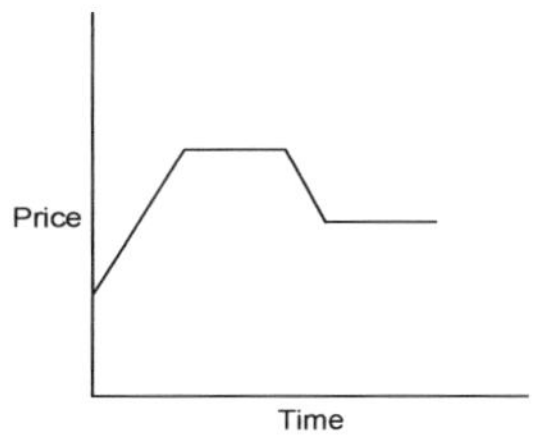

B.
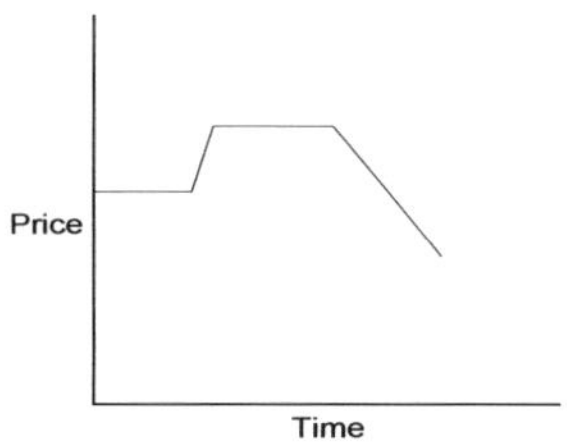

C.

D.

Your Notes

Question 18

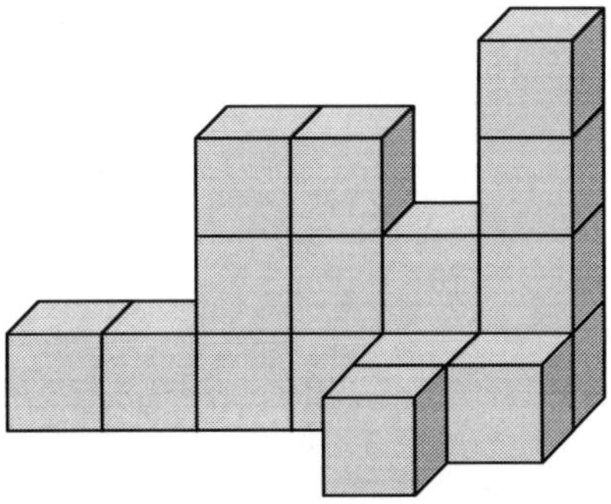

Which of the following represents the top view of the three dimensional figure shown above?

A.

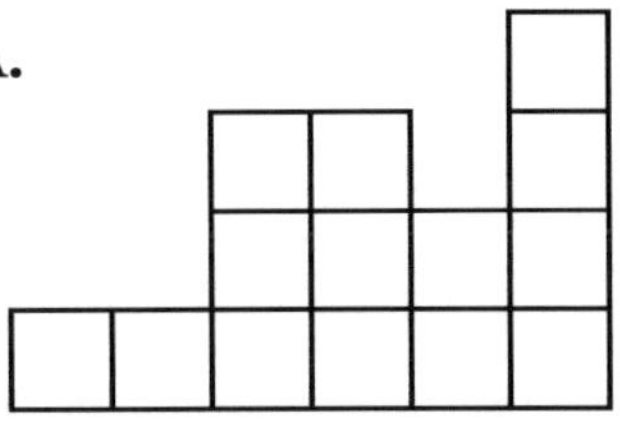

B.

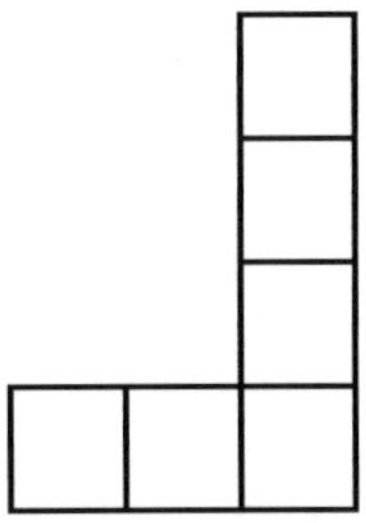

C.

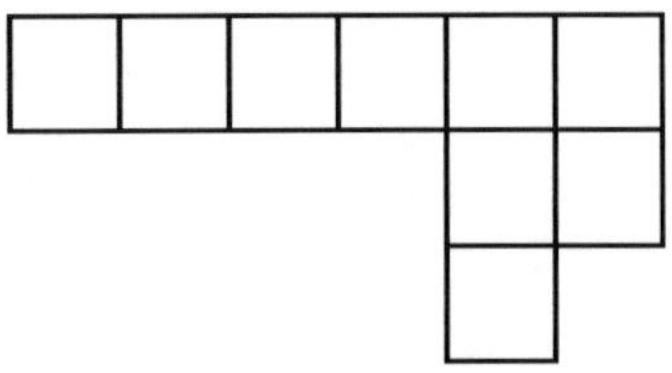

D. None of the above

Your Notes

Question 19

Your Notes

If the equation $y = x^2 + 1$ was changed to $y = 2x^2 + x + 1$, which of the following accurately describes some attributes of the change in the graph?

A. The graph will become narrower and shift to the left

B. The graph will become narrower and shift to the right

C. The graph will become wider and shift up the y-axis

D. The graph will become wider and shift down the y-axis

Question 20

What is the solution of the system of equations $2x - 3y = 7$ and $x + y = 6$?

A. $(6, 7)$ **B.** $(5, 1)$

C. $(-13, 19)$ **D.** $(1, 5)$

Question 21

Which of the following describes **every** line with an undefined slope?

A. The x-intercept is always 0

B. The slope is equal to 0

C. The line is horizontal

D. The line is vertical

Question 22

Last week the price of a gallon of gasoline was $2.15, this week a gallon of gasoline is 10% higher than it was last week. Next week the price of gas is expected to be 20% lower than this week's price. About how much is the expected price of gas for next week?

A. $1.89 **B.** $2.13

C. $1.50 **D.** $1.77

Your Notes

Question 23

Find the area of the regular pentagon, with side length, 2x, and apotherm, x-3, shown below.

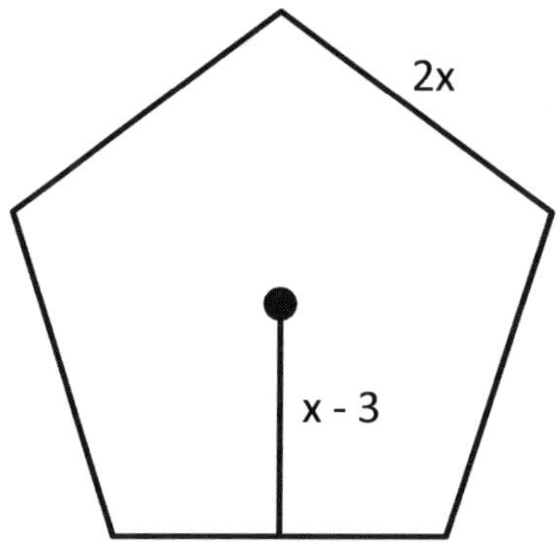

$$Area = \frac{1}{2}(apothem)(perimeter$$

A. $20x^2 - 60x$

B. $5x^2 - 15x$

C. $10x^2 - 30x$

D. $11x - 3$

Question 24

Which of the following lines forms a 90 degree angle with $-2x - 5y = 12$, and has a y-intercept of 4?

A. $y = \frac{5}{2}x + 4$

B. $y = \frac{2}{5}x - 4$

C. $y = -\frac{2}{5}x + 4$

D. $y = -\frac{5}{2}x + 4$

Your Notes

Question 25

Your Notes

The party host hid five gift boxes under five separate identical chairs. Each box is the same size, but each is a different color. The colors are blue, green, pink, red, and black. Also, in each box is a coin that was randomly placed to display either heads or tails. When the first guest arrives she selects a seat randomly from among the five chairs. What is the probability that under her chair there is a black box containing a coin displaying heads?

A. $\frac{2}{5}$ **B.** $\frac{1}{2}$

C. $\frac{1}{10}$ **D.** $\frac{1}{5}$

Question 26

Write the equation of the line that passes through $\left(-2,-4\frac{1}{2}\right)\left(\frac{1}{5},-1\frac{3}{4}\right)$.

A. $y = -4/5\,x + 3$ **B.** $y = 5/4\,x - 2$

C. $y = 4/5\,x - 2$ **D.** $y = -5/4\,x + 3$

Question 27

If the length of a rectangle is 14 inches and the width is 12.2 inches, about how long is its diagonal?

A. $15.6 in$ **B.** $18.6 in$

C. $26.2\ in$ **D.** $9.6 in$

Question 28

What would happen to the graph of the equation $3x^2 + 4x + 2$, if the three is changed to a five?

A. The graph will shift two units up

B. The graph will shift two units down

C. The graph will become wider

D. The graph will become narrower

Your Notes

Question 29

Which of the following **cannot** be a solution to the inequality $4x \geq 2y + 3$?

A. $(5,1)$

B. $\left(-1/4, -1/2\right)$

C. $\left(-1/3, -4\right)$

D. $(2,1)$

Question 30

A can of soup has a diameter of 11 centimeters. The height of the can is 7 centimeters. Find the area of the label surrounding the can. (use 3.14 for π) Round your answer to the nearest tenths place.

(Free response)

Your Notes

Question 31

Your Notes

What is the parent function of a linear equation?

A. $y = x + 1$ **B.** $y = |x|$

C. $y = x^2$ **D.** $y = x$

Question 32

Brittney made $142 on Tuesday from baby-sitting and will not receive anymore money until the weekend. On Wednesday, she spent $30 to get her hair done and she also spent $13.50 at the movies. If Brittney has $115 on Thursday, and she did not spend any more of her money, how much money did Brittney have before she made the $142 from baby-sitting?

A. $12.50 **B.** $13.00

C. $18.00 **D.** $16.50

Question 33

Which of the following is not a function?

A.

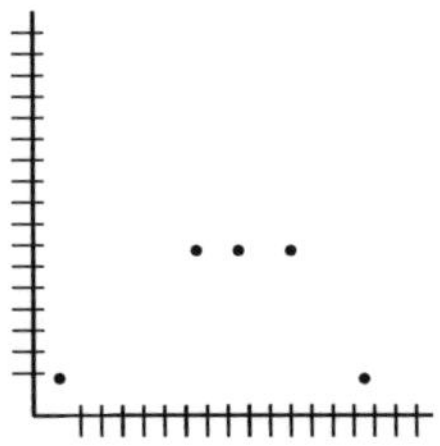

B.

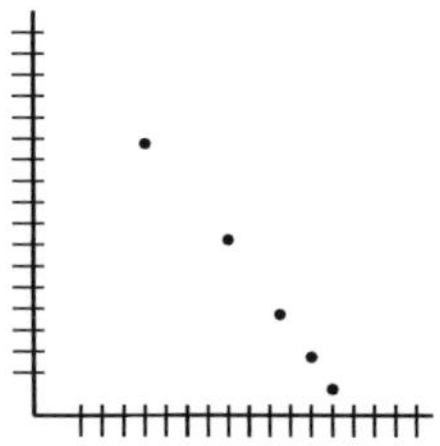

C.

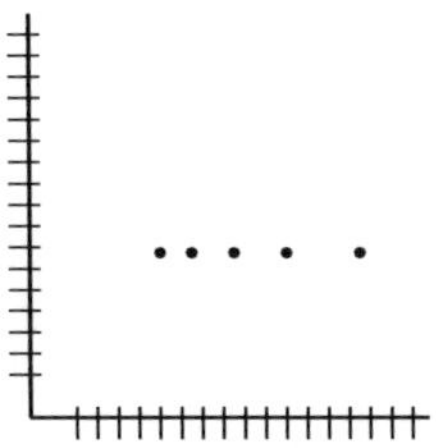

D.

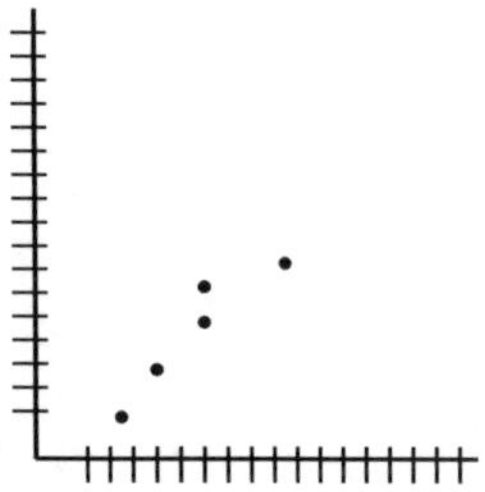

Question 34

What are the solutions to the function $x^2 + 7x + 12 = y$?

A. $(0,4)(0,3)$

B. $(0,-4)(-3,0)$

C. $(-4,0)(-3,0)$

D. $(3,0)(-4,0)$

Your Notes

Question 35

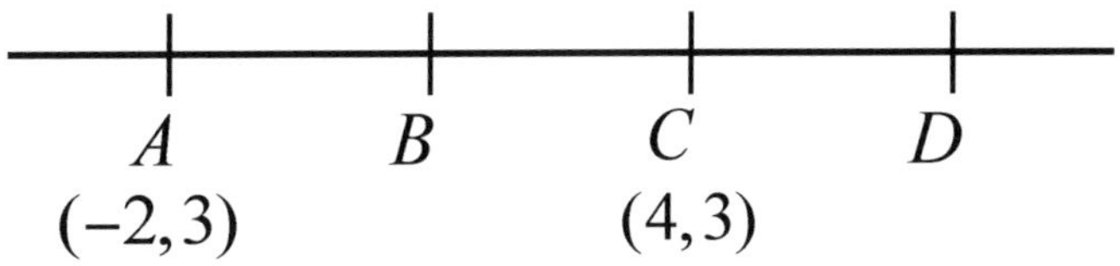

If $\overline{AB} \cong \overline{CD} \cong \overline{BC}$, how long is $\overline{AD}$?

A. $9 \, units$

B. $12 \, units$

C. $6 \, units$

D. $7 \, units$

Question 36

Which of the following equations corresponds to the chart shown below?

x	y
2	−2
5	25
7	53

A. $y = x^2 + 2x - 10$

B. $x = 2y - 6$

C. $x = y^2 - 10$

D. $y = x^2 - 6$

Your Notes

Question 37

Your Notes

Simplify the following expression: $m(3m-2)+(m+5)(m-2)$

A. $5m^2 - 10$

B. $4m^2 + m - 10$

C. $3m^2 + 5m + 10$

D. $6m - 10$

Question 38

There are 660 students in a school and all of the grade levels perform about the same academically. Of these students, thirty-three have straight A's. If the principal picks eighty students at random, about how many are probably are on the honor roll?

A. 4

B. 23

C. 10

D. 6

Question 39

Mary, John, Jasmine, and Dana all contributed a specific amount of money for their senior trip. Altogether they contributed $492. John contributed $36 and Mary contributed $72. What percent of the total did Jasmine and Dana contribute?

A. 22% **B.** 14%

C. 78% **D.** 69%

Question 40

Timothy has two similar boxes in his garage. The larger box has a volume of 64 cubic centimeters. The smaller box has a length ½ the size of the larger boxes length. What is the volume of the smaller box?

A. $32cm^3$ **B.** $8cm^3$

C. $16cm^3$ **D.** $128cm^3$

Your Notes

Question 41

Simplify the following: $(3x^2y^3)^2(2xy)$

A. $18x^5y^7$ **B.** $9x^4y^6$

C. $6x^5y^7$ **D.** $5x^4y^3$

Question 42

A square has a diagonal 25 inches long. What is the perimeter of the square?

A. $71\,inches$ **B.** $50\,inches$

C. $100\,inches$ **D.** $141\,inches$

Your Notes

Question 43

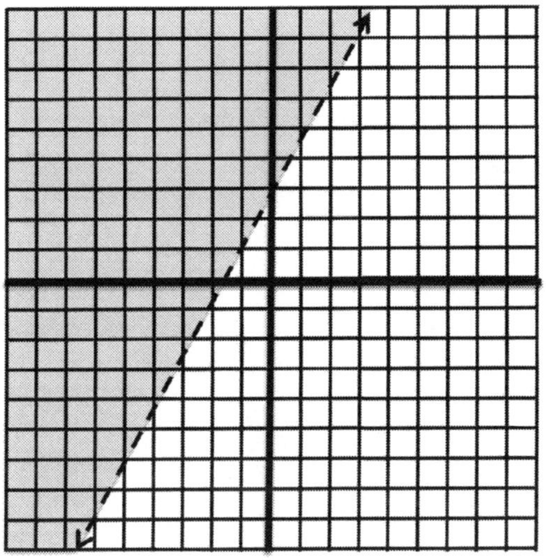

Which of the following best describes the inequality shown above?

A. $y > \frac{5}{3}x + 3$

B. $y < \frac{5}{3}x + 3$

C. $y > \frac{3}{5}x + 3$

D. $y \leq -\frac{3}{5}x + 3$

Your Notes

Question 44

Your Notes

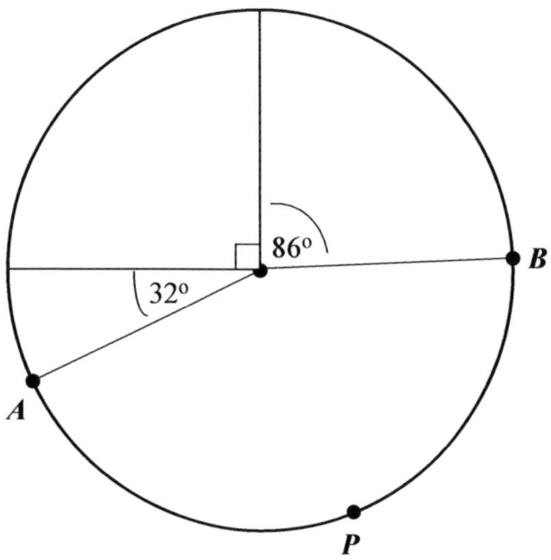

The distance from the center to point A for the circle shown above is 5 centimeters long. Which of the following is closet to the length of arc $\overparen{APB}$?

A. $152\,cm$

B. $13.3\,cm$

C. $11\,cm$

D. $7.9\,cm$

Question 45

Your Notes

A tire has a radius of 3.26 inches and is rolling on pavement. If the tire rolls through exactly 4 revolutions, what is the approximate total distance the tire will have traveled?

A. 133.55 *in.*

B. 40.97 *in.*

C. 20.47 *in.*

D. 81.93 *in.*

Question 46

A restaurant surveyed 50 customers, asking them which soup they liked better. Of the 50 people surveyed, 15 said they preferred Brand A soup, 10 preferred Brand B soup and the remaining didn't like any of the soups. Based on this, which conclusion can be drawn?

A. 50% of the customers preferred Brand B soup.

B. 10% preferred Brand B soup.

C. 20% preferred Brand B soup.

D. 15% preferred Brand A soup.

Question 47

Toni is cutting a circle from a square sheet of paper shown below. About how much paper will be left over after he cuts out the circle?

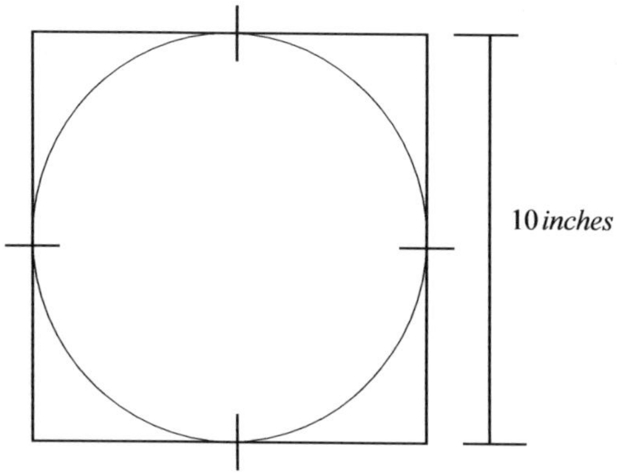

A. $21.5 in^2$

B. $31.4 in^2$

C. $78.5 in^2$

D. $68.6 in^2$

Question 48

The area of $\square ABCD$ is 144 inches, and the length of side AE is 17 inches. What is the length of $\overline{CE}$ in the figure shown below?

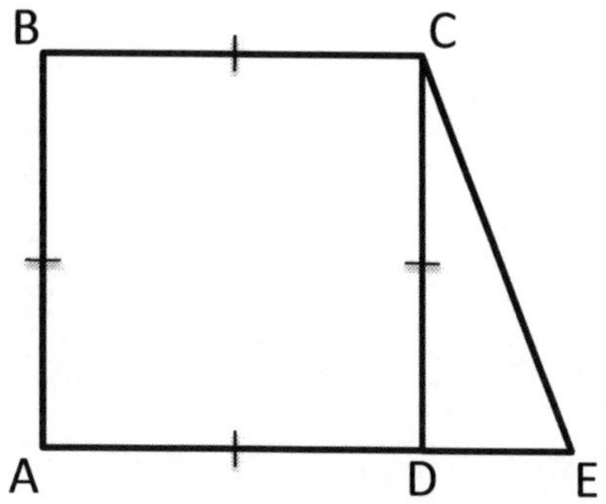

A. 5 *inches*

B. 13 *inches*

C. 12 *inches*

D. 24 *inches*

Your Notes

Question 49

Marquee High School has 450 students. There are 175 freshmen, 120 sophomores, 55 juniors, and the remainders of the students are seniors. What percentage of the students at Marquee High School are seniors. (Round your answer to the nearest tenths place)

Your Notes

Question 50

At Al's Grocery Supply Store, the cost of a bag of ice is directly proportional to its weight. If a nine pound bag of ice cost $3.00, about how much would a one hundred pound bag of ice cost?

A. $33.00

B. $27.00

C. $103.00

D. $300.00

(YOUR NOTES)

ANSWERS TO TEST 1

and Score Log

ASSIGN TWO POINTS FOR EVERY CORRECT ANSWER

RECORD YOUR SCORE HERE ____________________

DATE ______________

Answers to Test 1

1. D
2. B
3. D
4. A
5. D
6. C
7. C
8. C
9. C
10. A
11. D
12. D
13. A
14. B
15. A
16. D
17. A
18. C
19. A
20. B
21. D
22. A
23. B
24. A
25. C
26. B
27. B
28. D
29. B
30. 241.8 or 77π
31. D
32. D
33. D
34. C
35. A
36. A
37. B
38. A
39. C
40. B
41. A
42. A
43. A
44. B
45. D
46. C
47. A
48. B
49.22.2%
50. A

TEST 2

- TIMED TEST -

TOTAL TIME = 70 MINUTES (1 HOUR AND 10 MINUTES)

Question 1

What is the arc length that corresponds to a 40 degree central angle for a circle with a circumference of 9π inches?

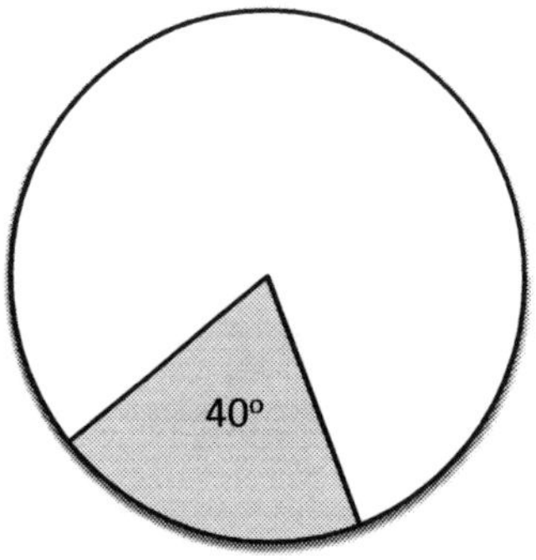

A. $\frac{10\pi}{9}$ *inches*

B. 10π *inches*

C. π *inches*

D. 11 *inches*

Question 2

Which of the following lines is perpendicular to $4x - 2y = 7$ and passes through the point (3,-2)?

A. $y = \frac{1}{2}x - 2$

B. $y = -\frac{1}{2}x - \frac{1}{2}$

C. $y = -3x + 2$

D. $y = \frac{-3}{2}x$

Your Notes

Question 3

Given a line with a slope of 0 that passes through the point (-4, 5), which of the following lines is perpendicular to this line?

A. $x = 10$

B. $x + y = -4$

C. $y = -5x + 4$

D. $y = x$

Question 4`

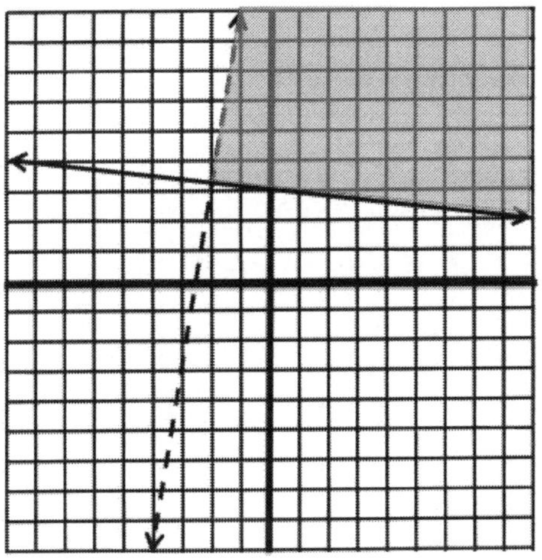

What system of equations describes the shaded area in the figure above?

A. $\begin{cases} y > 3x + 1 \\ y \geq 6x - 3 \end{cases}$

B. $\begin{cases} y \geq 6x + 15 \\ y < -\frac{1}{8} + 3 \end{cases}$

C. $\begin{cases} y < 6x + 15 \\ y \geq -\frac{1}{8} + 3 \end{cases}$

D. $\begin{cases} y \leq 8x + 15 \\ y < -\frac{1}{6} + 3 \end{cases}$

Your Notes

Question 5

If the graph of $y = x^2 - 8$ is changed to $y = \frac{1}{64}x^2$, which of the following will occur?

A. The graph will shift 64 units down, and become narrower

B. The graph will shift 8 units down, and become wider

C. The graph will shift 8 units up, and become wider

D. The graph will shift 8 units up, and become narrower

Question 6

Lisa Ann put her motorcycle on sale for $8,000, which was 20% below the price that she originally paid for it. However, she finally sold the motorcycle at a price that was a 15% discount from her asking price. Which equation could be used to find the difference between her original purchase cost and her eventual sales price?

A. $8000 * 0.20 – 8000 * 0.15

B. $8000 / 0.15 – $8000 / 0.20

C. $8000 / 0.80 – $8000 / 0.15

D. $8000 / 0.80 – $8000 * 0.15

Your Notes

Question 7

The table below lists the costs of model automobiles that Francisco has purchased. To complete the set he is interested in purchasing a model sedan, but must keep the average price for the entire set of models at or below $25 per item.

Model	Cost
Sports Car	$32
Jeep	$25
Truck	$41
Sedan	
SUV	$16
Mini Van	$12

What is the maximum price that he can pay for a model sedan?

A. $24

B. $21

C. 27.50

D. $26.25

Question 8

Gabriella has a poster that is in the shape of a perfect circle. However, it has a radius of 20 inches and she needs a poster with a radius of only 10 inches. About how much area will Gabriella need to cut away to reduce the poster to a circle of the desired size?

A. $312\,in^2$

B. $564\,in^2$

C. $795\,in^2$

D. $942\,in^2$

Your Notes

Question 9

Your Notes

The below pie chart describes the allocation of 200 marbles by color in a box.

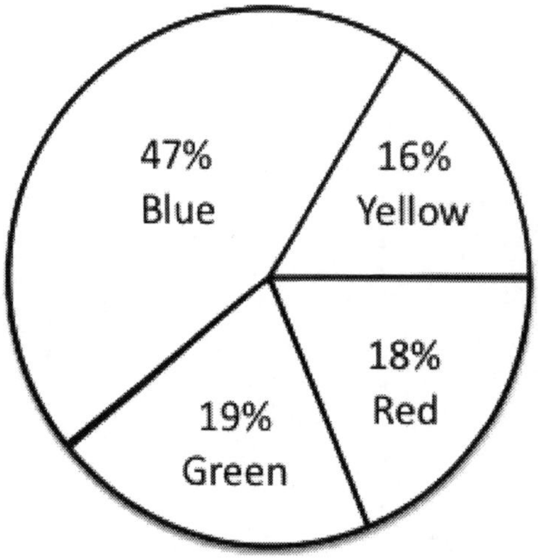

About how many degrees is the central angle corresponding to the blue marbles?

A. 47°

B. 120°

C. 169°

D. 241°

Question 10

Consider a right triangle with perpendicular legs of lengths 12m and 6 m. What is the perimeter of the triangle?

A. $18m$

B. $18 + 6\sqrt{3}\,m$

C. $31m$

D. $18\sqrt{18}$

Question 11

Simplify the following: $\dfrac{\left(2x^{6}y^{-5}m^{-4}\right)^{3}}{4\left(x^{3}y^{-2}m^{-2}\right)^{2}}$

A. $\dfrac{3x^{5}y^{7}m^{8}}{4}$

B. $\dfrac{2x^{12}}{y^{11}m^{8}}$

C. $\dfrac{x^{5}y^{11}m^{8}}{2}$

D. $\dfrac{2x^{3}m^{2}}{y^{7}}$

Question 12

A square has area 2. What is the length of the diagonal of the square?

A. 1

B. 2

C. 3

D. 4

Your Notes

Question 13

A special configuration of certain instruments can detect the elevation of the center of a cumulus cloud. When instrument A detects that it is directly under a cloud it sends a signal to instrument B which is located away from, but at the same elevation as instrument A. Instrument B then immedately from its vantage point detects the cloud's angle of eleveation with resepct to the elevation of the instruments A and B. This information is then sent to a computer that calculates the height of the cloud above instrument A.

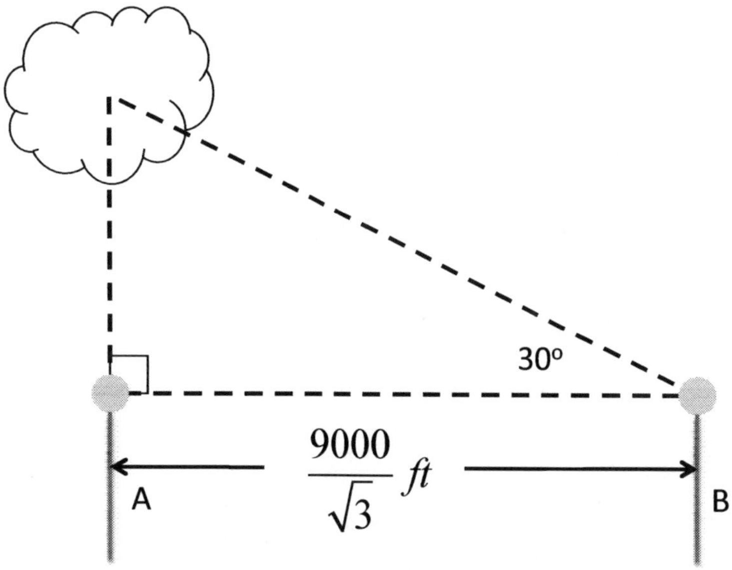

Given the distance from instrument A to instrument B, $\frac{9000}{\sqrt{3}}$, and the angle of elevation, 30°, in the figure above, what is the height of the cloud above instrument A?

A. $9000\,ft$

B. $\frac{4500}{\sqrt{2}}\,ft$

C. $4500\sqrt{2}\,ft$

D. $3000\,ft$

Your Notes

Question 14

Your Notes

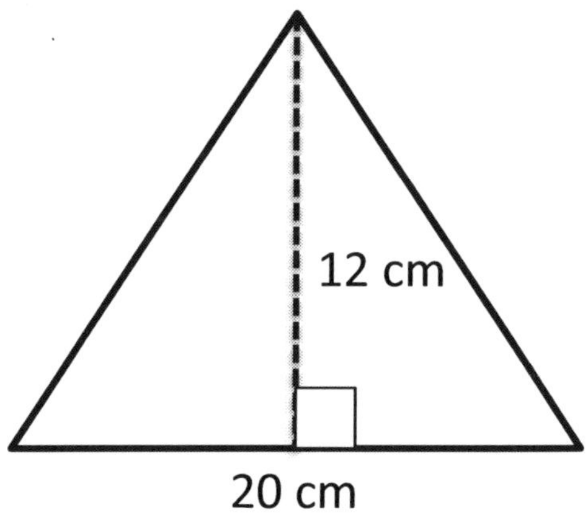

The figure above shows a triangle with base that measures 20 cm and a height of 12 cm. Which of the following is the area of a similar triangle that is $1\frac{1}{2}$ scale.

A. 270 cm^2

C. 45 cm^2

B. 90 cm^2

D. 180 cm^2

Question 15

Which of the following is included in the graph of $-3x + 2y \geq 14$?

A. (-3, -3)

B. (4, 2)

C. (2, 6)

D. (-2, 4)

Question 16

Your Notes

What is the y intercept of the line $4x - 3y = 3$?

A. -1 **B.** $-\frac{3}{4}$

C. $-\frac{4}{3}$ **D.** 3

Question 17

Jaworski Lawn Service charges a monthly fee of $80 for garden maintenance plus $50 per day for lawn mowing and grooming. Which of the below equations is useful for calculating the yearly cost of the service if lawn mowing and grooming will be required x times per year.

A. $c = 50x + 80$ **B.** $c = 960 + 50x$

C. $c = 80 - 12(50-x)$ **D.** $c = 80x + 50$

Question 18

What is the solution for the equations $5x - 3y = -2$ and $-4x + y = 3$?

A. $(\frac{4}{5}, 2)$ **B.** $(1, -1)$

C. $(-1, -1)$ **D.** $(1, 7)$

Question 19

Which equation below is the parent function of a quadratic equation?

A. $y = x + 1$ **B.** $y = |x|$

C. $y = x^2$ **D.** $y = x$

Question 20

A circle of perimeter 8π is located just inside of parallelogram $\square ABCD$ and tangent to sides $\overline{AB}$ and $\overline{CD}$.

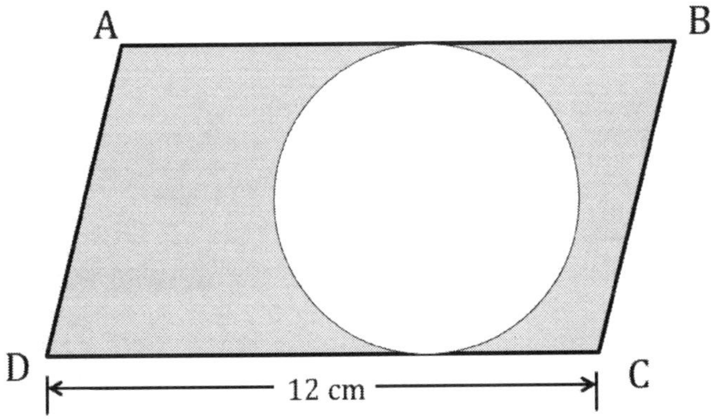

What is the area of the shaded region?

A. $96 - 8\pi$ **B.** $106 - 16\pi$

C. $96 - 16\pi$ **D.** $48 - 8\pi$

Your Notes

Question 21

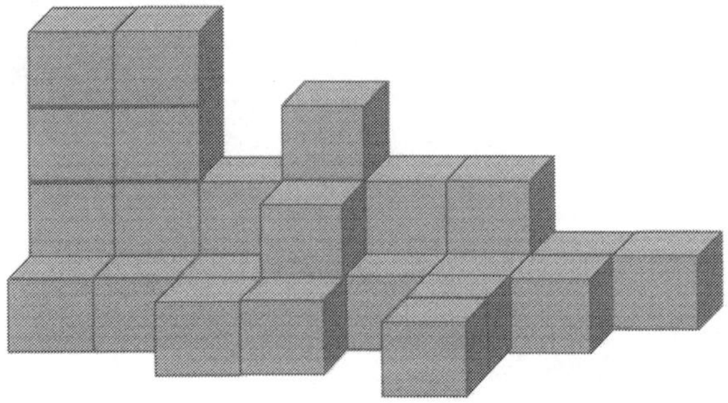

Which of the following represents the top view of the three dimensional figure shown above?

A.

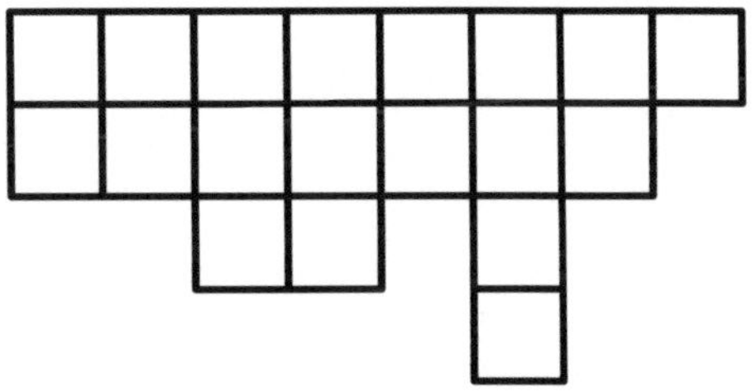

B.

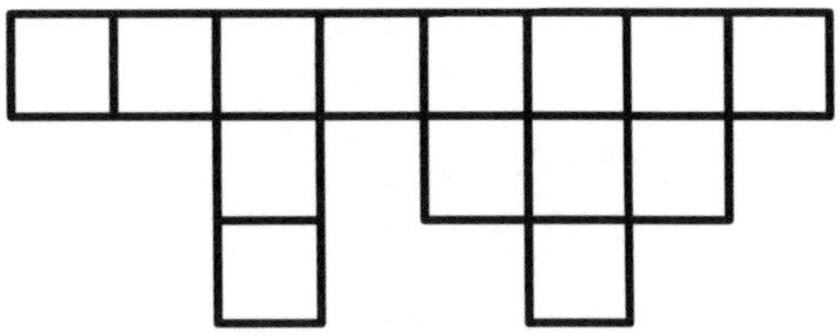

C.

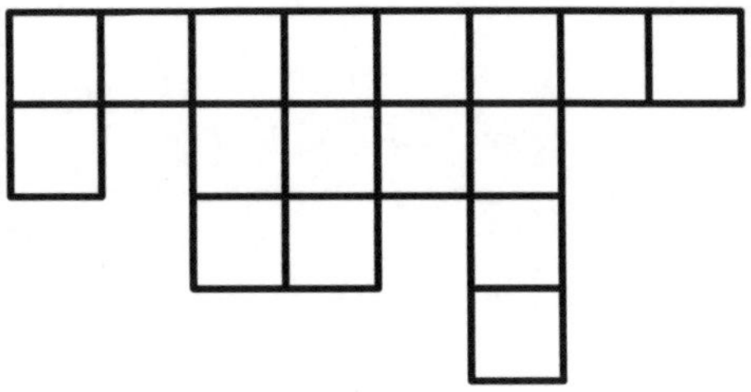

D. None of the above

Your Notes

Question 22

Your Notes

If the equation $f(x) = -2x^2 + 4x - 5$ is changed to $f(x) = 2x^2 + 2x - 5$, which of the following accurately describes attributes of the change in the corresponding graph?

A. The graph will open in opposite direction and shift to the left.

B. The graph will shift to the left.

C. The graph will open in the opposite direction and shift to the right.

D. The graph will shift to the right.

Question 23

A square has a diagonal 20 inches long. What is the area of the square?

A. 100 *sq. inches*

B. 200 *sq. inches*

C. $200\sqrt{2}$ *sq. inches*

D. $400\sqrt{2}$ *sq. inches*

Question 24

Which of the following describes **every** horizontal line?

A. The x-intercept is always 0

B. The slope is equal to 0

C. The slope is equal to 1

D. The line is perpendicular to the x-axis

Your Notes

Question 25

The annual budget for medical research at a local hospital was \$1,200,000 last year. The budget is \$900,000 this year. What is the percent of decrease?

A. 25.0%

B. 33.3%

C. 75.0%

D. 90.0%

Question 26

In the figure below, line l and m are parallel.

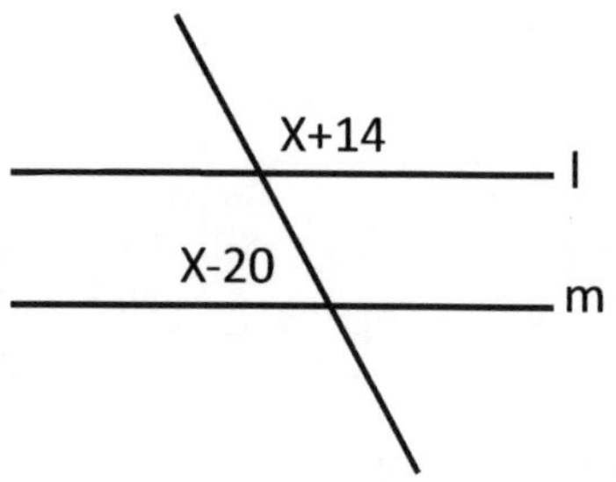

What is the value of x?

A. 104

B. 110

C. 76

D. 93

Question 27

Your Notes

Six girls are in a line-up in a televised modeling competition. To avoid elimination they must run to a far wall, select a pair of high heels shoes, run back to the line up in bare feet, and then slip the heels on and stand in the line-up again for ten minutes. The girls can choose between pink or black shoes. The producer for the television show has secretly made the pink shoes painful to wear and has decided to eliminate the girls that do not have big bright smiles after ten minutes in the line-up. If 4 of the 6 girls always prefer pink to black shoes, and half of the girls always cry or pout at the slightest pain or discomfort, then about how many girls should the producer expect to eliminate.

A. 1

B. 2

C. 3

D. 4

Question 28

Which of the below equations is of a line that passes through the points $\left(3,-\frac{2}{5}\right)$ *and* $\left(4,-1\right)$?

A. $y=\frac{3}{5}x-\frac{17}{5}$

B. $y=-\frac{3}{5}x+\frac{7}{5}$

C. $y=\frac{1}{5}x-\frac{1}{5}$

D. $y=\frac{1}{5}x+\frac{1}{5}$

Question 29

If the diagonal of a rectangle is 12 inches and its width is 5 inches, about how long is its length?

A. $11\,inches$ **B.** $17\,inches$

C. $7\,inches$ **D.** $13\,inches$

Question 30

What are the coordinates of the vertex of the parabola expressed by $f(x) = -3x^2 + 18x - 4$?

A. (-3, -85) **B.** (0, -4)

C. (3, 23) **D.** (2,20)

Question 31

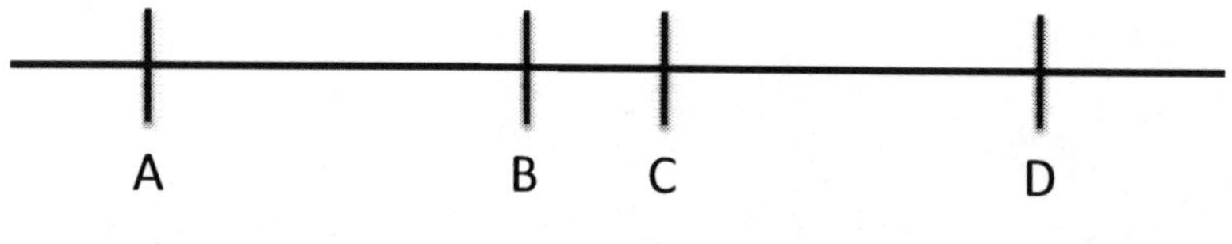

(Figure not to scale)

If $\overline{AC} \cong \overline{BD}$, $AC = 17$, and $AD = 22$, the how long is $\overline{BC}$?

A. 5 **B.** 10

C. 12 **D.** 17

Your Notes

Question 32

Which of the following is located on the line, $y = -4x + 15$?

A. $(-4,15)$ **B.** $(-1,15)$

C. $(15,0)$ **D.** $(2,7)$

Question 33

Brad made $29 per hour as a bouncer at a club. He also received 15% of the bar tips. On a standard 4 day week, he works 30 hours and shares in the bar tips that average $1000 per night. Which equation describes his standard weekly revenue?

A. $R = 0.15 * 29 * 30 + 4000$ **B.** $R = 29 * 30 - 0.15 * 4000$

C. $R = 29 * 30 + 0.15 * 4000$ **D.** $R = 29 * 30 + 0.15 * 1000$

Question 34

A cylindrical jar of radius 4 cm holds a maximum of 480π cm^3 of liquid. The jar was filled to capacity with blue dye. After the dye was pored out the interior surfaces of the jar were observed to be completely stained blue? Excluding the bottom surface of the jar, and assuming that the jar has no lid, what is the surface area (i.e. lateral surface area only) that is stained blue?

A. 240π cm^2 **B.** 160π cm^2

C. 120π cm^2 **D.** 64π cm^2

Your Notes

Question 35

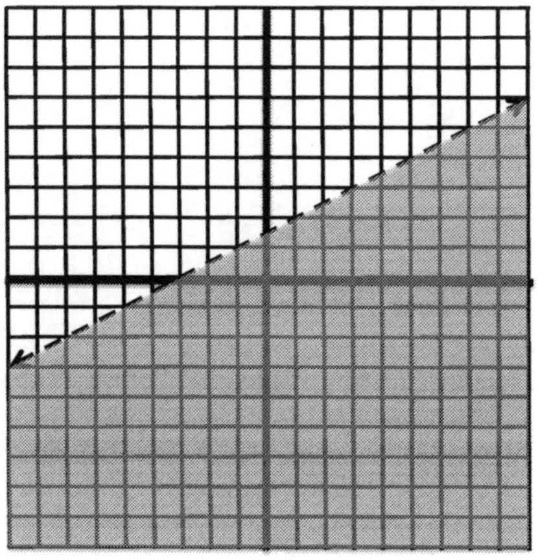

Which of the following best describes the inequality shown above?

A. $y < \frac{1}{2}x + \frac{3}{2}$

B. $y > -\frac{1}{2}x + \frac{1}{2}$

C. $y \leq \frac{1}{2}x + \frac{3}{2}$

D. $y > -\frac{1}{2}x + \frac{3}{2}$

Question 36

The cost of laundry service is directly proportional to the weight of the clothes. If it costs $15 to launder 50 lbs of clothes, how much would it cost to launder 245 lbs of clothes?

A. $816.67

B. $73.50

C. $750

D. $105.50

Your Notes

Question 37

Your Notes

Which of the following is not a function?

A.

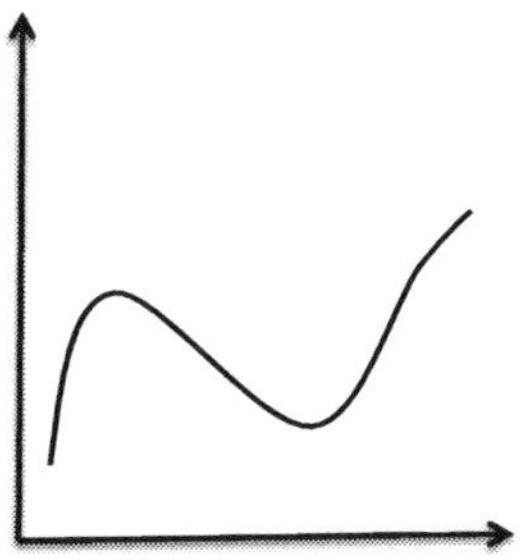

B.

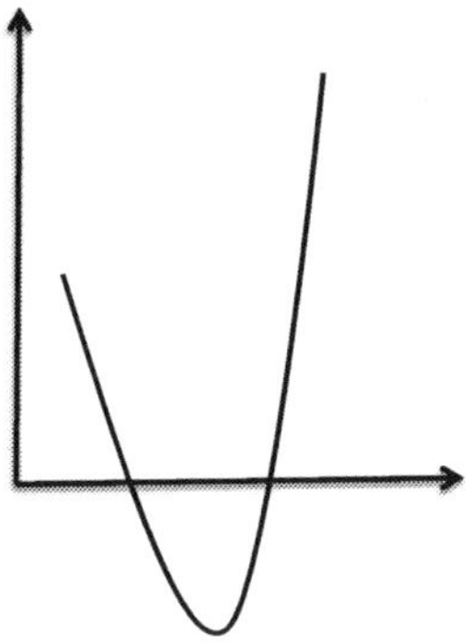

C.

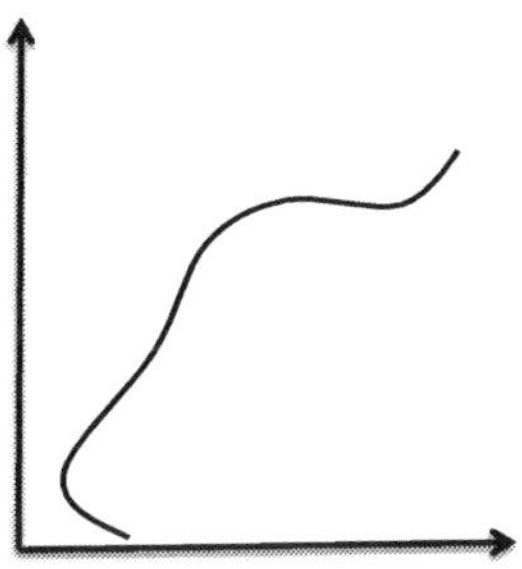

D.

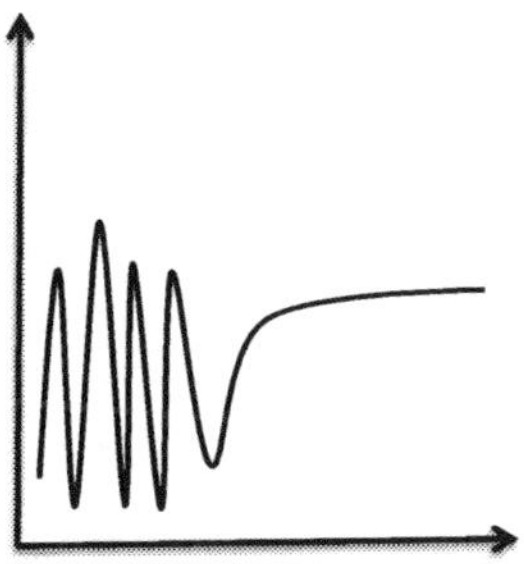

Question 38

Given the zeros of the function $f(x) = -2x^2 - 14x + 60$ are $(x_1,0)$ and $(x_2,0)$, what is the value of $x_1 + x_2$?

A. 4

B. 0

C. - 7

D. -13

Question 39

Simplify the following expression:

$4x + 3x - 2(5x - 2y) + x(5 - x) - 3(6 - 2x)$

A. $8x + 4y - x^2 - 18$

B. $x^2 - 6x + 4y - 18$

C. $-x - 4y - 18$

D. $-x^2 - 4x + 4y - 18$

Question 40

A certain pet store produced purchasing statistics based on customer behaviors. The store observed that 20% of pet adopters selected black animals. The store also observed that a forth of the people who adopted animals were also the only people to purchase leather collars. If the store sold 20 leather collars last month, then about how many people adopted black animals?

A. 10

B. 4

C. 16

D. Cannot be determined

Your Notes

Question 41

At the party the ratio of women that did not wear a hat to the women that wore a small hat was 5 to 3 and the ratio of women that wore a small hat to the women that wore a large hat was 2 to 7. Adrian counted 63 women wearing large hats at the party. How many women were at the party?

A. 189 **B.** 126

C. 146 **D.** 111

Question 42

Lathia's stylish suitcase has a maximum volume of 4 cubic feet. She needs more space for packing but wants all of her suitcases to match in the same style and color. Shopping online, she found a suitcase that is virtually identical, except that all of the dimensions are doubled. What is the volume of the new suitcase?

A. $8\,ft^3$ **B.** $12\,ft^3$

C. $16\,ft^3$ **D.** $32\,ft^3$

Your Notes

Question 43

Your Notes

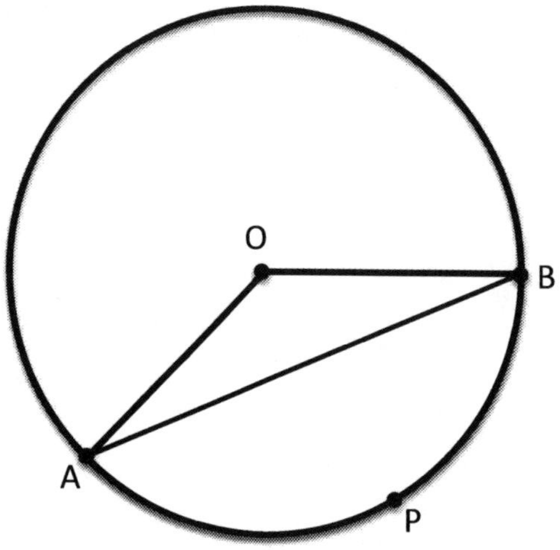

For circle O, the measure of $\angle OAB$ is 25°. What is the measure arc APB?

A. 25°

B. 50°

C. 130°

D. 240°

Question 44

How many square tiles, each 2 feet on a side, are required to completely cover a patio of dimensions 32 feet by 15 feet.

A. 672

B. 240

C. 120

D. 64

Question 45

A car tire rolls through exactly 40 revolutions in a straight line on flat pavement, causing it to travel 100 meters. What is the approximate diameter of the tire?

A. 1 m

B. 0.8 m

C. 1.2 m

D. 1.4 m

Question 46

The number of men voting in the election was twice the number of women voters. Among women voters, three times as many women voted in the morning than had voted in the afternoon. If 3000 women voted in the morning early, what was the total number of voters voting in the election.

A. 32,000

B. 24,000

C. 12,000

D. 8,000

Question 47

A store table hosts great sales on T-shirts that are being discontinued. The quantity of the colors available are 25 black, 15 red, 30 white, and 50 of mixed color designs. If the mixed color designs contain all of the colors of the other shirts, about what percent of the T-shirts on sale include the color red?

(Free response)

Your Notes

Question 48

Your Notes

Eloi earns $2000 per week for promoting events at various arenas. He is also paid an additional $4000 per event for each event that attracts more than 10,000 guests. Last year Eloi promoted events every week and attracted 180,000 guests to 30 events. Which of the following is needed to determine the amount of money that Eloi earned last year?

A. The number of months that had events

B. Which events had the highest number of paying guests

C. The average number of guests per event and the number of weeks that Eloi worked.

D. The number of events that were attended by 10,000 people or more

Question 49

Simplify the following: $(3x^4yz)^2(2xy^2z^3)$

A. $18x^9y^4z^5$

B. $6x^7y^4z^5y^2$

C. $9x^8y^4z^6$

D. $18x^5y^6z^5$

Question 50

A dog accelerates down a hill chasing a fast cat. The dog reaches a maximum speed and holds this for a few moments. Still going down the hill, the dog slows down because the cat has vanished in nearby bushes. Suddenly, the owner summons the dog, which despite being tired hurriedly scampers further down the hill toward the owner, running fast with renewed energy.

Which graph of speed versus time corresponds to the behavior of the dog in the described sequence?

A.

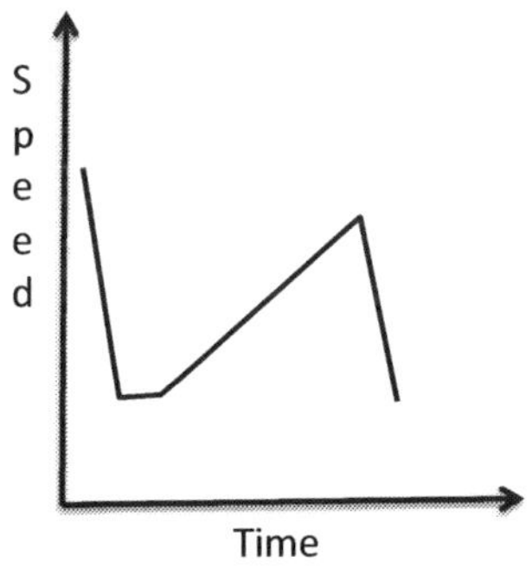

B.

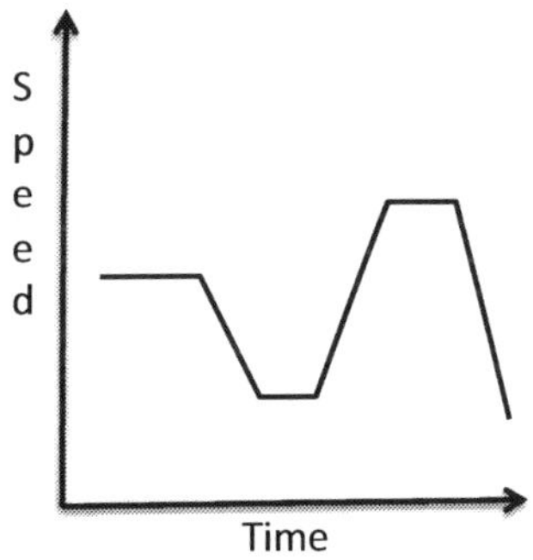

C.

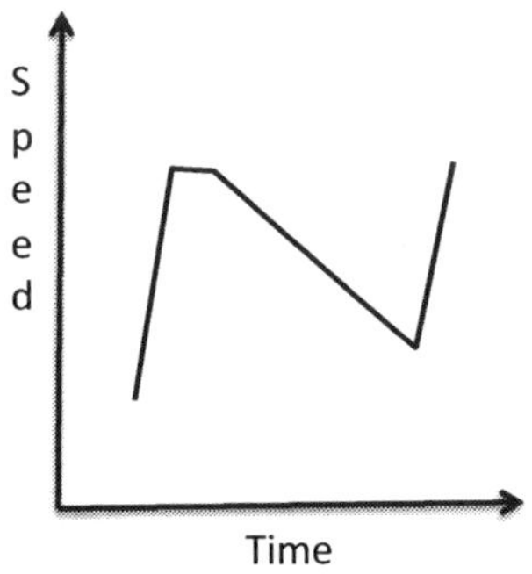

D.

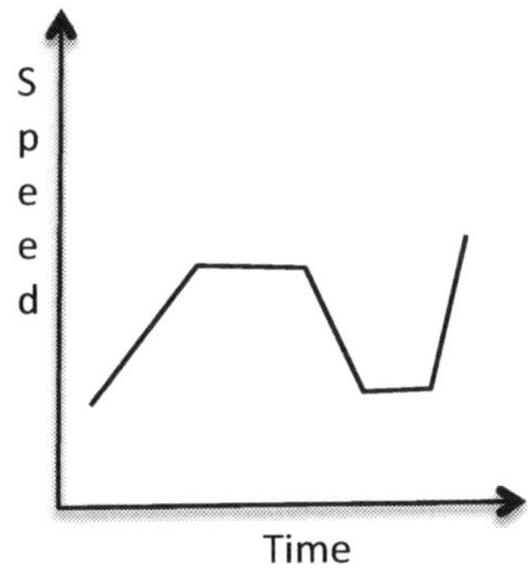

Your Notes

(YOUR NOTES)

ANSWERS TO TEST 2

and Score Log

ASSIGN TWO POINTS FOR EVERY CORRECT ANSWER

RECORD YOUR SCORE HERE _______________

DATE ___________

Answers to Test 2

1. C
2. B
3. A
4. C
5. C
6. D
7. A
8. D
9. C
10. C
11. B
12. B
13. D
14. D
15. D
16. A
17. B
18. C
19. C
20. C
21. A
22. A
23. B
24. B
25. A
26. D
27. B
28. D
29. A
30. C
31. C
32. D
33. C
34. A
35. A
36. B
37. C
38. C
39. A
40. C
41. D
42. D
43. C
44. C
45. B
46. C
47. 54.2%
48. D
49. A
50. C

(YOUR NOTES)

(YOUR NOTES)

36032524R00097

Made in the USA
Middletown, DE
22 October 2016